MW00680743

NEVER LUCY

A Journey of Trials, Triumphs, and Gifts of the Spirit

LETICIA WALKER

Never Lucy

A Journey of Trials, Triumphs, and Gifts of the Spirit by Leticia Walker

Print IBSN: 978-1-54391-368-2

eBook ISBN: 978-1-54391-369-9

TABLE OF CONTENTS

Dedication

I REMEMBER THAT WHEN I WAS A CHILD, I WANTED TO BE A WAIT-
ress when I grew up because waitresses gave food to people, made you laugh,
and had a uniform. Later, I wanted to be a nun, even though no one in my
family was Catholic, because I liked the uniform. As I got older, I thought
maybe a therapist; a lawyer or a nurse would be okay. These were all day jobs,
of course, because I was always going to be an entertainer. This could explain
why, as a nursing major, most of my courses were music related.

In my youth, I was told that I would not amount to anything in life
because I had too many irons in the fire, too many interests. In high school,
the teacher that I most admired, my music teacher, told me to give up music,
my passion, because I was more suited for a job in the area of service like a
teacher or a nurse. He explained that since I learned to read music in high
school, I was too far behind the other kids who had been singing and playing
instruments since they were small children.

I dedicate this book to all the people who were and are able to erase
the negative messages they were given and move forward. I dedicate this book
to all people who have been abused and celebrate with the people who have
risen above it and learned that they deserve to be loved. We all deserve love.

I dedicate this book to Donna, and our children, Jayson, Shawn and
Jeremy who have helped me to remember that love in its purest form is perfect, forgiving and endless.

Preface

I woke up this morning to the sound of John Legend's *All of Me* playing in my head. Somehow, it was September 21, 2014 again.

I saw the processional in my mind's eye. The guys were so handsome in their black suits, white shirts and purple ties. The ladies were flawless in their stunning purple gowns, styled to fit the uniqueness of each woman. The flower girl was elegant in her purple dress, carrying a white basket filled with purple and green rose petals. The ring bearer was regal, dressed like the men, rocking the same purple tie sized just for him. Clearly understanding the importance of the task at hand, with poise and grace, he carried the rings on a white satin pillow trimmed in lace.

Then a bride—radiant, breathtaking. A circle of flowers delicately placed on her head with a trailing veil flowing, she walked down the aisle with one of her three very handsome sons.

I heard words and music. The choral group sounded like angels delivering God's blessing. It was indeed a day to remember: a lifetime coming and it had arrived!

I sighed at the recessional, while Stevie Wonder summed up the event: *I'll be loving you always.*

Part I

Whisper From God

I LOVE SITTING OUTSIDE ON THE BACK PORCH FROM MID-MORN-ing till about two in the afternoon. The sun is high in the sky and dazzling bright. Everything that is green is so green. It can be so peaceful. I love closing my eyes and feeling the sun on my face. Often the sun is countered by a gentle breeze, like a whisper from God.

Days like this remind me of times gone by: grape Kool-Aid and pretzel sticks, mud pies made from real mud and wild onions that I cooked in my Easy Bake oven. I loved playing kickball, Hide-N-Go-Seek, Color Forms, Barbie dolls, and putting on shows for my mom. I even had a black Chatty Kathy.

However, my favorite doll was "Coffee Coolers". She had coffee colored skin and pursed red lips. Her lips had a small hole in them. When you squeezed her, air came from her mouth as if she were blowing on something to cool it. Fifty years later as I write this, I am just realizing the correlation between her name and her talent. Don't know how I missed that. I guess at the time kids just accepted what was, especially Christian kids. I can still hear my mom saying, "God first, others second, and me last", words I still live by.

I remember that I was a very busy kid. I had Girl Scouts, Sunshine Girls—sort of like Girl Scouts for Christians—, dance class, a fan club for a local band, volunteer work with the blind association, school, and YWCA.

I wonder why I never noticed bad things that happened to me, things that I never talked about when they happened. Was I afraid or did I not understand how awful it was, how wrong? I think I just lived in a world that only let in the good stuff, fun things. If it made me feel bad or weird, I erased it. But it never really goes away.

It is so quiet and peaceful sitting on the back porch watching the sun bounce off the rippling water in the pool; and nature, in all its splendor is like a big hug. Greeting me are dragonflies, butterflies, birds and chipmunks. Purple petunias and vinca add color to a wooded backdrop of very tall trees. The birds sing a familiar song that I don't know but love to hear. And there it is: that gentle breeze, a whisper from God.

Everyone is Welcome

MY MOTHER AND GRANDMOTHER MOVED TO ALLENTOWN AFTER
my grandfather died in the late forty's. He died before I was born. My grandfather was a cattle dealer and a musician. His band, The Colored Fun Makers,
was quite popular locally. I am told he was the largest cattle dealer in Lehigh
and Northampton Counties. My grandparents owned three farms; one of
them was at the foot of the Blue Mountains.

Sadly, unscrupulous lawyers took advantage of my mother and grandmother, who were not business savvy and knew very little about my grandfather's business dealings. My grandfather's shares in Abbotts Dairy, which later
became part of Lehigh Valley Dairy, were gone along with other family assets.
Some of which we believe were simply signed away because my grandmother
trusted the wrong people.

My mother still longs for country life. She told me that where she grew
up everyone was the same and got along. My grandfather had all kinds of
people that worked for him. My mother didn't experience racism until she
got to Allentown.

My grandmother bought a home across the way from our house. This
made it easier for mom to look after her, and Grammy could maintain her
independence. In the early 1960s, we lived in a five-bedroom row house on
Lehigh Street in Allentown, Pennsylvania. Mom painted the front porch bat-
tleship gray. Then she hand-painted twelve perfectly matching red diamonds

on the mantel on top of the three-quarter cement wall that surrounded the porch. I always knew which house was mine, even in the snow.

My parents were separated when I was three months old. My sister, Catherine, was eleven years older than me. We did not play well together. My mom told me that when I was an infant, my sister put me in a dresser drawer and closed it. She did not want a baby sister. My mother heard me crying and came to my rescue. Growing up, my sister and I were not close. In fact, we were always fighting, but I loved her. One day after school, we were arguing, as usual, about a Beatles record. My sister was watching me till mom got home from the store. She had a nosebleed, told me she was dying, that the small blood clot was her brains falling out, and that it was my fault. I was so scared and didn't know what to do. So I ran back to the school crossing to get my friend Stella, the crossing guard. Stella was a very nice lady. She had blonde hair that was styled like Sally Rodger's hair in the Dick Van Dyke Show. She often wore a black and yellow hat similar to a policeman's hat, an orange vest, and a big yellow raincoat that was always open. I told Stella that my sister was dying, and she ran back to the house with me to help my sister. Much to our surprise we found my sister in the kitchen getting a snack. There was no blood in sight. She thought it was funny. Stella went back to her post, and my sister yelled at me for getting Stella. Then she laughed at me. I told mom, and she just told us to stop fighting. My sister and I continued to argue. I called her a bitch. She told mom, and mom promptly canceled my upcoming camping trip with my Girl Scout troop. Even now this all seems a bit twisted to me. I got punished, but my older sister didn't and she started the fight. I only called her a word I heard in the street. I didn't even know what it meant. I just knew it was what other kids said when they were fighting. Mom told me that a bitch was a dog. So I got grounded because I called my sister a dog. It did not seem fair to me.

Sometime later, I was coming down the stairs and found my sister and her boyfriend fighting in the foyer. He had both her hands in his grip; they were yelling, and my sister was trying to get away from him. I quickly jumped over the last few steps, picked up the broom that was standing in the corner, and started beating him over the head. He had to let her go to try to stop me from beating him. Instead of helping me, or going for help, my sister yelled at me and told me to stop hitting him. He left, yelling that I was a crazy brat, and my sister was mad at me for saving her from this guy who was clearly hurting her. As if that wasn't enough, as he left he knocked over a glass windowpane that was leaning against the wall. It broke and hit my leg. By this time mom came home just in time to remove the glass from my leg and stop the bleeding. I still have the scar.

When my sister got her first car, I was not allowed in it. She would take the foster kids for a ride or to the store with her, but not me. I never really understood any of this. My mother told me that my sister treated me this way because she was jealous that I looked like her, and my sister looked like my dad. Mom let me go out a lot just so she had some peace from the fighting. I had Girl Scouts, a few neighborhood kids, and my friends. We often played in the parking lot till dusk. If the lightening bugs were out you had best be at least in the yard.

As I grew up, there were moments that my sister and I were at least civil to each other. However, even after she had children of her own, our relationship was strained at best. My sister, for the most part, kept me from having a real relationship with my nephews when they were kids. There were no outings with Aunt Tish, not even on outings with my kids.

However, all this changed when Grammy got sick.

While on a visit with our grandmother at the hospital, my sister and I were forced into reality. Grammy was very sick. However, even till the end, she was Grammy. She scolded us and told us that she was worried about our mom and that it was killing our mother that we didn't get along. She said she wanted us to bury the hatchet right then and there and not in each other's back. She said it was time we acted like sisters. She asked us to promise her we would stop fighting and get along. We both said we would. That wasn't good enough for Grammy. She made us shake hands over her in her hospital bed. We did. It took time but we built a real loving relationship. It was complicated at times, but real. Grammy would be happy and proud.

My mother was a foster parent and took care of children in our home. There was always a baby around. Mom loved babies. Sometimes my cousins stayed with us. We were all raised as brother and sister. My mom made it work and we never wanted for anything.

On Sunday's we had dinners with all the trimmings, almost like a holiday. After dinner we would sometimes play games, but we always played music and danced. Music was always playing at our house. My cousins were in a band that rehearsed at our house sometimes, Jay and the Techniques. It seemed like everyone in our family had a talent. It was my mother who taught me my first tap steps. She was a dancer with my grandfather's band when she was very young. My uncle, her brother Tommy, played guitar. We called him the Rock and roll trash man because he was always singing while he worked. He was in grand pops band too. He was my favorite uncle.

There was an ESSO gas station less than a mile down the road from our house. If you stood close to the street in front of our house, you could see it and its tall landmark sign. In 1963, gas sold there for twenty-nine cents a gallon. The week before Christmas, Mom and I would bundle up and take the extremely cold and very snowy walk down to the gas station to get our Christmas tree. It was a big event and fun. I loved my winter coat; it was candy apple red with black and white trim and mittens and red boots to match. The snow was halfway up my boots and still coming down as we walked down the street.

The gas station was set up like a fair. There were white lights strung all around the place. The lights were very pretty against the night sky, and with the snow falling down, they twinkled even more. Christmas trees were everywhere leaning on wooden workhorses. We picked out our tree, and the man tied it up for us. Mom and I each grabbed onto the tree where we could and dragged it all the way back to our house, digging a trail along the way. The snow came down heavier and heavier as we walked. When we got home, we shook all the snow off the tree so that we could bring it into the house. We got out of our drenched and snowy clothing and enjoyed hot chocolate and cookies.

Every Christmas, Mom baked chocolate chip, peanut butter, butter cookies and sometimes, ginger snaps. Christmas time was cookie time at our house, and I loved it.

I loved decorating the tree. Mom always put lots of colored lights on the tree. She also hung tinsel, angel hair, and sometimes candy canes. For the holidays, we always had chocolate candy, chocolate covered nuts and creams of all kinds, and ribbon candy. We always had a lot of fruit at Christmas time, especially big fruit baskets and fruit arrangements on the table with cookies and candy to decorate them.

Christmas dinner was a feast for a king. We had a huge twenty-six-pound turkey, two kinds of stuffing, regular bread stuffing and clam stuffing, which my mother loved. We had mashed potatoes, sweet potatoes, gravy, corn, creamed peas with carrots, cranberry sauce and dinner rolls. Dessert was outrageous. There was apple pie, pumpkin pie or peach cobbler and, of course, cookies and candy. Sometimes she made rice pudding. My mom would never buy ready-made rice pudding. My mother never got ready-made or store-bought anything.

Mom loved nativity scenes. We always had a beautiful manger scene on the mantle in the living room and outside for the holidays. Mom had a manger scene on the front lawn that she added to during the year. After Christmas and when winter was over, she would add three crucifixes in preparation for Easter and a tomb complete with a stone that could be rolled away on Easter morning. She made all these things herself. She was very crafty. She decorated the outside of the house as much as the inside. There were lights and garland everywhere. People would drive by our house just to see the decorations and the lights on the house.

I remember, one Christmas there was a knock at the door. The family had just sat down to dinner. The table was full of everything Christmas dinner should be.

"Go answer the door, Tish," Mom told me, and so I did.

There stood a man I'd never seen before. He was dressed in ragged dirty clothes, and the dirt on his hands and face was visible.

"Mom? Uh, come here, please," I called out. She came right away.

"I'm hungry, ma'am," the man said. "Could I have some food?" Clearly, he hadn't had anything to eat in a while, a long while.

"Won't you come in and join us?" Mom said much to my surprise, although, she could have given him food to go.

As he walked into the house, I immediately smelled a putrid odor coming from him. He needed a bath. My mother invited him to join us for Christmas dinner. She directed him to a place where he could wash his hands. When he returned to the table, she directed him to sit right next to me. I mean, I wanted to eat, but that smell! Mom led us in prayer. The stranger bowed his head as if he was giving thanks too. It must have been nice to get out of the cold for a while. The dinner table was oddly quiet except for: "Pass me the ham please; can I have the turkey please?"

I asked the stranger if he wanted some creamed peas and carrots, a holiday favorite at our house. He took the spoon and put some on his very full plate. He was not being greedy. Everyone's plate was full. Mom was quite a cook, and she went all out at Christmas.

"How about a fresh baked roll?" I questioned.

"Thank you ma'am," he said.

I smiled and giggled. No one had ever called me ma'am before.

He finished his plate, commenting on how good the food was, thanked the family, and smiled. After dinner, my mother packed him a doggy bag full of everything we had for our Christmas dinner and also some cookies and candy. He thanked us and went on about his business.

We never saw or heard from him again. But I never forgot how my mother took a complete stranger—smelly at that—into our home, shared our Christmas holiday with him, and gave him food for a later time. I am reminded of that part of the Bible that talks about Christ knocking on the door: "When I was hungry, you gave me food." It appeared that this man had no one in his life and nowhere to go, but he somehow was led to our house, where everyone was welcome . . . always.

That's how it is at my house now, years later. Everyone is welcome.

School Daze

I LOVED SCHOOL. ELEMENTARY GRADES WERE FUN. WE HAD GAME time, snack time, recess; and on Wednesday afternoons, we left the school building, walked two blocks to a church, and the whole class went to church school. Even learning was fun. Everything became a game. I can still recite the Preamble to The Constitution. Kids seemed to like me. I don't remember being at a loss for friends.

When I was in the second grade, two of the boys cornered me in the coatroom and groped me. I got away from them and went into the classroom as if nothing happened. The truth is I didn't really know what happened. I just knew it made me feel odd, different. Later, some of the kids teased me that boys wanted to be my boyfriend. What does that mean when you are seven?

In the fourth grade, my teacher, whom I adored—in a fit of what I now call stupidity—wrote everyone's name and weight on the blackboard for all to see. She left it up there for weeks. It changed the way a lot of the kids treated me. Now I had unpleasant nicknames and constant references to my weight.

Mr. Cigar

WHEN I WAS EIGHT, I WENT TO A BLIND ASSOCIATION MONTHLY meeting with my mom and Grammy. I got to tour the place where my Grammy worked, which was downstairs from where the meetings were held. Grammy was totally blind, but it seemed she could do just about anything. Her friend, the president of the organization, offered to show me exactly where my grandmother's workstation was and what she did. Mom and Grammy stayed upstairs in the meeting room, so they could help with refreshments.

Mr. Cigar, as I called him, who reeked of cigar because he was always smoking one, took me downstairs. It was very dark and smelled like graham crackers and milk. He knew where the lights were, went right to them, and turned some of them on. I thought this was so amazing because he was blind, and also this wasn't his house. I didn't know about legally blind. People who are legally blind often have some sight, but not twenty-twenty vision, even with corrective visual aids.

I saw where they caned chairs, made rugs, and packaged plastic utensils. They even assembled garters. Across the room, the lights were not as bright. There was a big wooden seat, like a throne that a king would sit on. Mr. Cigar went to the seat and sat down. He called me away from the chair caning area and over to him. I went. He picked me up, sat me on his lap and gave me some red licorice candy. We chatted about school, my dolls and all kinds of stuff. Then he put his hand under my dress, moved my panties to the side and touched me. I continued to eat my candy and the conversation went on as if nothing was happening.

"Do you like ice cream?" he asked.

"Yes, vanilla," I replied.

"What toys do you like?"

"I like my dolls, I have three of them," I replied. I felt scared and suddenly alone, like I was in a dungeon. The lack of lighting on this side of the room created shadows and only added to my fear. The windows were covered. Does it hurt, he asked? No, I replied. I felt nothing, like he wasn't touching me.

After a while he stopped. He told me that I shouldn't tell anyone, not even my mom. He said it was our secret. He gave me a fifty-cent piece. I never told.

After that, when we went to meetings, I only went in the meeting room and the kitchen. When it was offered to me to go downstairs where Grammy worked, I declined.

I didn't understand why, but I knew I didn't want to go anywhere with Mr. Cigar, especially downstairs. No one ever asked me why, and I was not talking. As the entertainment, I often sang a song after the meetings, mostly church songs or a standard. They often asked me to sing *Moon River* or *More*. I also helped serve refreshments. Sometimes I passed out napkins. These were my jobs, and I made sure I was busy.

Mom often picked up other blind people to bring them to meetings. My grandmother always rode in the front—shotgun. I, being the kid, sat in the back seat with Grammy's friends—her blind, often male friends. On this particular day, I sat between two blind men, Frank and Jimmy. Frank was very tall and skinny. He didn't talk much. Jimmy was short and kind of hunched over, even when he walked. He was one of Grammy's best friends. Jimmy talked endlessly.

With my mom driving and my grandmother in the front seat, Jimmy slid his hand up my dress. I was able to block him with my arm and hand long enough. We arrived at the Blind Association, so he had to stop. You know he talked to my mom and Grammy the whole time he was trying to touch me.

I acted as if nothing ever happened. I never spoke of it. I felt cold. I felt nothing.

Later that year my mother sent me to give a package to Gracie, a family friend. Gracie was not home. She lived with Eddie, her man. He and some buddies were playing cards. I gave Eddie the package. He laid it on the table, grabbed my hand and spun me around as if we were dancing. His friends were laughing. He stroked my shoulder. I pulled away. The sound of the men laughing grew louder in my head. Suddenly, I was terrified. I had a bad feeling.

Then a voice of reason, one of the men yelled out, "Let her go Eddie!"

I ran out of there as fast as I could. I was beginning to think there was something wrong with me. Why do people want to touch me? It seemed everybody did, especially grownups.

Friends, Got to Have Them

I HAD TWO BEST FRIENDS WHO WERE SISTERS, WANDA AND Gladys. Their parents were very strict, and they were Jehovah Witnesses. My friends could rarely come to my house because their father did not like them socializing with people outside their faith. However, their mother was more open and understood what it was like for kids who are raised as Jehovah Witnesses, so I could go to theirs when dad was not home. Once in a while, I was there when he was. But it was rare. I had other friends, but there was that ever-present racial issue, so I spent little time at the homes of the kids and friends I went to school with. Wanda and Gladys were Hispanic, so race was not a big thing to their parents. They were the only Hispanic family in the neighborhood.

I didn't have a lot of black friends. The black kids didn't like me. They often called me names. I remember a time when a group of kids jumped me on the way home from school. They pushed me down, hit and kicked me.

"You think you are better than we are?" They would say.

"You think you're white. White nigger."

I can still hear them taunting me as I write this. I went home bleeding with scraped knees and a flood of tears.

Mom said they picked on me because they were jealous. Of what? The next day my mom went to see the principal about what happened. Her visit to the school did not improve things for me with the kids.

17

I decided to try to make peace with some of the kids who taunted me. I wanted them to stop picking on me. I wanted them to like me. Mom told me that I could invite some of them over to play. I had a swing set and a small roller coaster in the backyard. The roller coaster had four steps to climb. Once at the top I would get in the car and ride up the small slope and down the other side very fast. I had no shortage of things to play with. My mom was the perfect mom, very involved in what I was doing, even school. Their moms—not at all involved.

Some neighbors had parties for grown-ups at their homes all the time with lots of drinking and fighting. I wasn't allowed to go any of their houses. It seemed like every week the cops were at the house at the end of the block. Knives and guns were involved as well as something called running numbers that, to this day, I do not understand.

Mom saw to it that whenever I had kids over, there was snacks, drinks and fun. Kids would come to the fence to watch me and my new friends play, and want to join in. During the summer, I had a wading pool. That was a big draw. Sometimes we made a fort out of blankets. We would often turn the back porch into a stage and hang sheets to make a curtain, so we could put on shows. In the winter, mom helped me make an igloo-fort, which was huge fun.

However, the kids still were not that friendly when I wasn't entertaining them. Mom would say, "Not everyone that smiles in your face is your friend. You have fair weather friends, Leticia."

Mom loved kids, but not the type that were starting to be around a lot. I wasn't allowed to have more than five kids over at a time. Sometimes the kids at the fence would spit at us or call us names. They had to wait their turn. There were just too many to have over at one time. When my mom came out, they would run away. The first time mom told the kids that they couldn't come in for snacks and play, I became a lot less popular. She wasn't being mean. She needed a break because she did have other things that kept her busy.

One day I went to the house that the cops visited. I was trying to get along and be a part of the group. The kids invited me to play house. Finally, it was working. I was both happy and surprised. I knew I was not supposed to go in their house, so I didn't tell mom. She just thought I was outside playing in the lot where kids would often go to jump rope or play ball.

I had never played house without dolls. They took me to a bedroom and told me I could be the mom. It was an honor to be my mom. One of the girls was the dad, and she got to yell at the kids. She made them get on the floor and go to bed. She told me to sit on the bed.

I was the only fifth grader with boobs. They wanted to see them, touch them. They told me that this is what moms and dads do. The girl who was the dad, lifted my shirt, squeezed one and giggled. I didn't like their way of playing house. I told them I had to get home.

Good thing, because later that same day, the cops came and took their dad away. Someone had been stabbed there.

My two best friends, Wanda and Gladys, were so much easier. We laughed all the time. They had no interest in my body parts. We played games I understood, and we put on shows. We sang and danced when their father wasn't at home or when they came to my house. It was hard for them to be kids and Jehovah Witnesses. They had few, if any, celebrations. I wasn't allowed to give them gifts, not for their birthdays or Christmas, or ever. Their mom liked me. Their dad, not so much, because I wasn't like them.

My ears were the exception to the lack of interest in my body parts. They both had pierced ears. I didn't, and Wanda and Gladys thought that I should. After a while, I agreed. One day after school, we ran home to their house. We had a needle and a match to sterilize it with. They said it wouldn't hurt or even bleed. After all they had seen their mother do it many times.

She had done it to them. I closed my eyes . . . nothing. I didn't feel a thing. That's because she didn't do a thing. She got scared. We decided to ask her mom to help.

"Is it okay with your mom?" Mrs. Espodas asked.

"Of course," I said. "She won't care."

So she wiped my ears with alcohol and threaded a needle. She held the needle in the flame from the match, rubbed my ears with ice, and POW! Pierced ears. I had string in my ears for a week. Mom was not so happy when she saw what I had done. She cared.

Four doors down from my friends, Wanda and Gladys, lived a little girl named Rosie. My friends and I would sometimes throw a ball with her or sing songs. We often watched her when her dad was at work and her mom wanted to run to the store. Our families became friends. Sometimes I brought Rosie to our house. They lived just across the Charles Chip parking lot behind our house.

Rosie's mom, Maggie, liked to play bingo. Every weekend, there was a bus that picked people up to go play. Rosie's dad, Ray, often worked on cars behind his house on weekends for extra money. He didn't have time to watch the kids. Rosie had a baby brother, Thor. Maggie offered me a job babysitting while she went to bingo. Mom said it was okay for me to be the weekend babysitter.

I was so happy. It was perfect for me. I was only twelve but I could cook, change diapers, do the dishes and laundry all for two to five dollars, depending on what I got done. Plus, I got to take care of the kids, just like my mom did. Mom was a foster parent and was always taking care of someone else's kids.

The best thing about working there was the music. Often, I would turn on music and Rosie, Thor and I would dance. Everything was done to music: cooking, laundry, playing games. Sometimes, Rosie's dad and his friend, John, would come inside when they took a break or finished working on cars. We ordered steak sandwiches for lunch and danced. John was just out of high school. I don't know how he got to work on cars and be friends with Ray. I didn't like him much. I didn't know why.

I was good at my job. I sometimes made tuna salad for lunch, pork chops, potatoes, and corn for dinner. They didn't have a mixer. I had to mash potatoes with a potato masher by hand. I folded the clothes just right. The kids were always clean, fed and in bed by 8:00 p.m. Sometimes when I got there, the baby would not be changed and have diaper rash. I knew just what to do because I had seen mom care for kids all the time. I often thought that I took better care of the kids than their mother did. I think Rosie's father agreed. He told me when he was teaching me to slow dance.

"You're going to make someone a great wife one day," he said. He held me tight, very close, and we danced till the song was finished.

I liked him. He was one of my best friends. He also thought I was pretty. He told me so. He was pretty too. He was white with shiny black hair.

One Saturday, I came to work just like always. I went upstairs to check on Thor. He was in his parents' room in the front of the house. His crib was across the room from the bed. It was a nice room with two large windows facing the street. There was a vanity with a big mirror between the windows. Thor needed his diaper changed. The music was going, and I was singing along. I went into the adjoining room to get a Pamper, so I didn't notice that John, Ray's friend, had come into the house and upstairs.

"Oh, hello," I said when I did notice him, and then I started to walk back to the crib. He pulled me from behind and pulled me back into the adjoining room, onto the bed. I began to fight him. I tried to get him off me. He was just too big. He was tall and fit. As I struggled, I began to cry. Ray came in. He grabbed John, pulled him off me, punched him and kicked him out, literally, kicking him down the stairs.

"Get the hell out my house, and don't ever bring your black ass around here again," he yelled.

I ran into the room where the baby was in his crib and stood near the window. I saw John walk down the street, limping. I was crying uncontrollably. Ray came into the room, walked over and put his arms around me. He patted me on the back, trying to console me. He pulled me to the vanity, still hugging me. He sat down, pulling me closer to him. Still crying, I was shaking.

"Come, sit down," he said as he guided me toward the bed.

I sat on the edge of the bed. He stood in front of me. Ray held my hand and dried my tears. Then he touched my leg. I moved his hand. He took my hands, raised them over my head as he pushed me back on the bed. I started to cry again.

"No! Please no, you saved me. No, the baby," I pleaded. Two-year-old Thor was in his crib watching like it was a TV show. Rosie was playing in the yard.

I clenched my knees together. He forced them apart with his legs. With his free hand, he ripped my underwear and used his body to spread my legs further. I tried to scream. It wouldn't come out loud.

"Shut up or I'll throw you out the window," he threatened. "Are you hot yet?

Are you hot?"

"Yes," I replied. "Yes, I need air. Open a window."

He laughed and ignored my request.

"I want to make a woman out of you," he kept saying. "I want to make a woman out of you"

"I don't want to be a woman," I kept repeating through my tears. "I don't want to be a woman."

In the background, I could hear the song, *A Whiter Shade of Pale,* playing on the radio. I called for my mom. I kept calling till I had no more voice. She never came. He finished and left me lying on the bed.

When I was able to, I got up, my knees hurting. I was dripping a mixture of blood and semen. I had a bruise on my forehead. I didn't know how I got it. I cleaned myself up, changed the baby and went downstairs.

Ray was sitting at the bottom of the steps. "If you tell your mother, she will know it was your fault; she will know what you did," he warned.

I went to the kitchen to get dinner, fighting tears, not knowing what to do. He was right, I couldn't tell my mother. Ray told me to make him a cup of coffee. I did. I looked over and saw a bottle of Bayer aspirin. I took two and poured the rest into his coffee. For a brief moment, I wanted him dead. I put dinner on the table. Ray accidentally knocked over the coffee.

I went home, leaving him with his kids and a mess to clean. I told my mom that I bumped my head on the kitchen cabinet. I balled up my torn panties and put them deep in the trash. I took a bath for what seemed like a lifetime.

For years I beat myself up. It was not because I believed it was my fault, but because I didn't hate him. I still don't hate him. I wanted to. This takes turning the other cheek to a new high. I didn't want to be a Christian. I wanted to hate. I just couldn't. I was very confused. He did a bad thing. I was pretty sure of that. Did that mean he was a bad person? Before this, he was my friend. He saved me.

Years later, I thought that I should find him and tell him that I know how to do it now. I know what, "Are you hot yet?" means. I know and understand what he did to me. He would never understand the enormity of what he did to me, how it colors everything, how it would affect my life, what I think and how I feel, and others around me. No one could.

The Doctor and Daddy

I MANAGED TO SOMEHOW PUT ALL OF THIS OUT OF MY MIND. IT was as if it never happened. Ray never told me he was sorry. Instead he told me he loved me. What had happened was not part of my reality most of the time. I just felt a sense of loss, like I was lost. I remember my teacher, Mr. Brong, telling my mom at parent teacher conference that he was concerned about my behavior at school. He said that while I was physically present in class, I always seemed detached and somewhere else. He could see that I was not paying attention. However, every time he called on me with a question, I gave the correct answer.

When September came, I moved up a grade in school. Junior high was very different from elementary school. They gave you a schedule to follow that mapped out your whole day of studies. You moved from class to class to a different teacher for each subject. My school had two floors.

Soon after the start of the new term, I had a terrible accident. I was coming from a class on the second floor. Halfway down the stairs, I fell. Someone ran for help and just like that I was on a cot in the nurses' office. The nurse made sure that I was ok. I told her my back hurt. She examined me, then called my mother. The nurse said that I needed to see a doctor. My mom came to pick me up. After she had a brief meeting with the school nurse, we went home.

When we got home, my mother became very talkative and had lots of questions for me that I didn't understand at first. She asked if there was anything that I wanted to tell her. Did I have a boyfriend? Then she told me that the school nurse told her that I was pregnant. I was in shock. *Did I hear her right? Can this even happen to me? How did this happen? I just passed my thirteenth birthday.* She had questions that I wasn't sure I could answer. It all happened so fast. Then I began to cry.

I had to tell her about that awful night several months ago when babysitting went all wrong. I had to talk about the night I took a bath for what seemed like a lifetime but never got clean. I had come home with a limp from my legs being forced open and a bruise on my forehead. It was all there in my head, even the lie I had told her and the memory of burying my ripped soiled underwear. It was not a good day. Mom blamed herself for letting me babysit and trusting a neighbor, allegedly, a friend. She made a doctor's appointment for me right away with her gynecologist whom she had not seen since I was born.

Next thing I knew, we were seeing a gynecologist. I had never been to this kind of doctor and had no idea what was happening to me. The doctor had me climb up on his exam table. It was different than my regular doctor's table. There were little metal cup-like things attached to the table on either side. The doctor told me to put my feet in them and slide down. "Bring your bottom to the edge of the table," he said. He stuck something inside me. It hurt, and it was awful. I didn't know exactly what he was looking for or doing. I was scared. I laid very still and quiet on the table but wanted to scream.

Then he came to the other end of the table to talk to me. The doctor slapped me across the face and asked, "How could you do this to your mother?" Later he told my mother that I would either be a homosexual or a hooker. *What a jerk!*

The doctor joined my mom in the next room. I could hear them talking, and the doctor was giving mom the business about not having seen a doctor since my birth, not even a follow-up after I was born. Mom caved in and allowed the doctor to examine her in another room. Turns out that she needed to have some polyps removed. There was so much happening. Within a four-week period, my mom had surgery that saved her life, and I gave birth.

Mom was kind and tried to preserve what was left of my childhood. The baby was three months old before mom could bring herself to have the talk with me, yes the sex talk. I wish it had been sooner. It was hard to understand what I was going through. I didn't fully understand what happened.

When I went into labor I thought I was dying. I believed that God was punishing me. I had so many questions. I was so thirsty and in excruciating pain. They would only give me a cool wet washrag to wet my lips and an ice chip. I delivered the baby without medication or an episiotomy. I had thirty-two stiches. I did feel oddly special and awful at the same time. I was fairly sure that God was not happy with me either. Still, it seemed that God took something really bad and made it good. I had a baby boy, a true blessing. After all, mom was better after her polyp surgery, and if I hadn't become pregnant, I never would have gone to the doctor and neither would she.

Mom thought it was important to tell my estranged father what happened to me. I didn't see why. It wasn't like he cared. My father had visitation rights. Every week, I was forced to go to his house, which was stupid because clearly he didn't want me there anymore than I wanted to be there. Stupid courts. When I rang the bell, he rarely answered. His girlfriend did. She would take me in the kitchen, give me a snack and sit with me until it was time to leave. He mostly stayed on his couch watching TV.

However, on this particular day, his girlfriend was not at home. My father actually answered the door and greeted me. I should have known something was up. He said he knew what happened, and he was sorry it happened. He hugged me. Then he took my face in his hands and proceeded to shove his tongue down my throat. I gagged. It was awful. His tongue was cold and thin. My head was spinning. It was beyond gross. We struggled. I pulled away and ran for the door.

"If you are going to give it away, you might as well give it to me," he yelled as I sprinted out of there.

I had no place in my brain to put any of this. I never went back. I didn't attend his funeral some years later. My mom didn't get it. I didn't and still don't hate him. Just didn't want to be near him, alive or dead.

Apparently, most of the men in my family agreed with the doctor and leaned toward the theory that I would be a hooker or a whore. It wasn't long after my father tried to rape me that my aunt's boyfriend would try. He was like an uncle to me. He lived with my aunt for years. We called him Uncle Walt. They didn't visit that often, but when they did Grammy was so happy. Aunt Clara was her oldest daughter and my mom's big sister.

On this particular visit, Uncle Walt decided to go upstairs using the excuse that he needed to use the bathroom. When he got to the top of the stairs, I was coming down the hall and passed him. Without a word, he grabbed me, pinned me against the wall and put his hand up my dress. I felt him push his fingers inside me as I tried to fight him. I got away. I won this battle and couldn't wait to tell my mom what he did to me so she would kick him out of our house and never let him back in. I went right downstairs and told my mom, Grammy and Aunt Clara what happened.

"You liar!" Aunt Clara yelled. I was shocked. "You wild kid. No good kid. Already had one baby. Get to your room. Making up shit like that. Get to your room."

My mom and Grammy talked to my aunt and Walt who lied through his teeth. So much for telling my mom stuff that happens to me when it happens to me, I thought. I was so mad and hurt that they believed him over me. I ran away . . . for about eight hours, until I got cold and hungry.

When I came home, my mom explained that they did believe me but had to pretend to side with my aunt and uncle because there was a chance my aunt would not visit Grammy again. I am sure it made it easier to believe me after my uncle George's girlfriend explained that Uncle Walt had tried to feel her up under the table.

The experience still smarts a bit after all these years. It is not what my uncle did that was so painful. It was what my mother didn't do. She didn't believe me. After everything she had said to me, after we found out that I was pregnant, about being able to talk to her and tell her anything, how if I had come to her in the first place things might have turned out differently, didn't ring true. I remembered that one of the things mom said when we talked about the pregnancy didn't make me feel very loved or supported in that moment either. Suddenly her saying to me that adoption for my baby was out of the question because it wouldn't look right to others that she is a foster mother but wouldn't keep her own grandchild gave me cause for pause, more to think about. Mom was angry—at the situation, me, herself, Ray, the world.

Grammy

My Grammy died in May of 1975. I loved Grammy so much. She was Welsh. She had smooth, creamy, beige skin and very soft hands. I loved to hug and kiss her. She would shush me away and say, "You are the *kissingest* kid I ever met! Kissing bug all the time."

Grammy was blind, but you could eat off her floors. Her house was always immaculate. She could cook or bake anything. She knew where everything was in her house. You better not leave a glass on her sink where she could knock it off. She would come after you with her cane.

"Run if you want," she would say. "You'll be still sometime." Yes, she would get you.

I used to love having breakfast with her: a cup of Tetley tea and toast. She would also eat half of a grapefruit, but not me.

Grammy was funny. She had some favorite sayings like, *there's a lid for every pot.* I remember bringing my boyfriend, Bob, home to meet her. Bob was concerned that she might have issues because he was white. When he met her, and we talked, she told us that, "If color rubbed off, there would be a lot of white guys running around with black dicks."

At the time, Grammy was the closest person to me who had passed on. I couldn't believe it. She was just gone. I had been sure that our whole family would go together when it was time. That way no one would be left to grieve anyone. My mom had spoken of it. I thought that God would take care of everything. I always believed that He would do something for me or give me a gift to make up for all the pain and craziness in my life. At the age of nineteen, I had endured so much in my life. It wasn't all supposed to be bad. But now Grammy was gone on top of everything else. I didn't know what to make of any of this life. This must be why we have faith, I thought, but my faith was dwindling.

Six years later, my all-time favorite movie, *Arthur*, was released. Liza Minnelli's character said she thought that the moon followed her. When I first heard this line in the movie, I immediately recognized myself in her character. I had been waiting for my turn, for God to make it up to me. I had lost so much.

The thing that bothered me the most was that I never got to choose whether or not I wanted to have sex or with whom. Being a virgin—that was stolen from me. My friends talked about marriage and what their first time would be like. No one ever described their first time as rape. They all seemed to know whom they would do it with.

The moon followed me, and I was special. Something wonderful would happen for me. God would make it right. So I waited.

Part II

Bastions of Bigotry

I REMEMBER GOING TO WOOLWORTH'S FIVE AND DIME TO APPLY for a job at the soda fountain. I filled out the application. The woman told me they didn't have any openings. I told her that I was answering the ad from the morning paper.

"Oh that job is filled," she said, "but I will keep your application on file."

I left and joined my girlfriend who waited for me outside. She pointed out that there was still a Help Wanted sign in the window. Then she had a brilliant idea. We walked back to the store. This time she went in, and I waited outside. She filled out the application. The woman spoke to her for five minutes, took the sign out of the window, and gave her the job. While sitting at the counter, my friend noticed my application lying in the trash.

Then there was the day the minister at the Baptist church I was attending at the time, took me aside, into his office after service. I was very involved with church projects, many of them with his son who had become a close friend. He proceeded to explain to me that God made oceans, mountains, rivers and streams to keep people where they belong and the races separate. He explained that God did not want the races to mix.

He questioned me about my friendship with his son and went on to say, "You should stay away because it isn't going to go anywhere."

When I ran out of the room in tears, he sent two deacons after me. They continued the humiliation by badgering me and asking, "Do you pray to God for a white man?" *You can't make this stuff up.*

High school brought other challenges. We lived in an area that had no diversity until we moved there. There were twenty-three blacks in a school of two or three thousand kids. I tried to fit in, but they only let me in so far.

I wanted to take college prep classes. My guidance counselor advised me to take general studies and typing. I loved music and wanted to pursue a career in that area but was advised to look for a career in a service area as I had no classical training under my belt at sixteen. I could sing but didn't learn to read music until high school. My musical peers had been playing instruments and studying music since they were in grade school. Many of them were involved in Community Theater and other musical and performance opportunities that were not available to me growing up. If there was ever any doubt of the reason that some opportunities were not available to me, it became very clear to me later on.

I did have a few friends in my high school days, and we made the best of high school. I dated a little. I even dated a class officer for a few months. Of course, it was a secret. He was white.

My very best friend, Cindy, was Jewish and lived two blocks farther west from my house. We spent a lot of time together and walked home from school together almost every day. I remember one day walking home from school with Cindy as usual, but things were different. Her grandmother had come to live with them. She was not as progressive as Cindy's father. Now instead of waiting on the front porch for my friend, I had to wait in the street. I couldn't even be on the public sidewalk in front of her house. I was so used to this kind of treatment that I completely accepted it. It was just another day in my world.

There was a time when my friends and I were going out for the evening. We took my car because I was the only one who had one at the time. I worked a full-time job at a local nursing home as a nurse's aide while in school and bought the car with my own money. My date had forgotten his wallet at the country club where he worked as a bus boy. On our way to pick it up, we had to make a stop to change seats. There were no blacks allowed at the country club unless you worked there. Black employees had to use the service entrance around back.

I didn't work there, so I got out of the driver's seat of my car. I got on the floor in the back of my car with coats piled over me so that I wouldn't be seen. It was tight as my friends were sitting in the back seat. We drove through the gate undetected. My date used the front door since he was white and his parents were members of the country club. He got his wallet, and we were off. My friends seemed to think this was funny. I felt less than—humiliated, unattractive, used and a bit hurt that no one in the car seemed to realize what I had to go through for my date to get his wallet. I never let on how I felt. It wasn't my best date.

But I did get to have my day a few years later. I was singing with a band that got booked for a wedding at that same country club. Decked out in a full-length sequined gown, covered by my luscious fur coat, I walked in through the front door and there wasn't a thing they could do about it. That did feel good, I must say.

I attended a local college that was presenting the musical, *You're a Good Man Charlie Brown*. I auditioned for the part of Lucy. I loved the show and knew the music going in. When the parts were posted, I was shocked by the choice they made for Lucy.

The person they chose wasn't known for her vocal abilities. The professor in charge could see my disappointment. She asked to speak to me after class. What she said summed up a lot of my life to that point, and going forward.

34

"Leticia, I am so sorry I can't give you the part. Your audition was wonderful."

Then the words came that have stayed with me all this time and always.

"But I can't have a black Lucy kissing a white Linus. You understand, don't you?"

I smiled, nodded, and took comfort in the fact that I could have been Lucy if I were white.

And then, a flood of memories came to remind me that I would never be Lucy in any situation. Ever.

The Three B's: Blonde, Blue, Bob

I MET BOB THROUGH A TEACHER WHO LED A YOUTH GROUP AT A local Methodist church. I went every week. It was fun. There was prayer and Bible study to enrich our spirits. We played games and had chats to build social skills. I made some new friends. Bob was one of them. Bob was not like the other boys in the group. He actually treated me like he treated everyone else, seemingly unaware that I was an overweight black girl, the only person of color in the group. The other kids barely talked to me at first; the girls, not at all.

Bob was a blonde-haired, blue-eyed German. He was tall and thin, but not skinny. We became best friends. We enjoyed youth group so much and worked together so well that they appointed us co-group leaders. We helped plan the activities and the Bible studies for our weekly meeting and activities for the younger kids. I don't really know how I became Bob's girlfriend. It just happened. Of course, it was a secret. Only three or four people knew. Racism runs rampant, then and now. So Bob and I only saw each other on Wednesdays and Sundays, during and after church activities. It was the after-church activities that got us in a bind.

The relationship went south when Bob's mom got a call that her son was hanging out with the wrong kind of girl and that I was pregnant. The caller clearly had not told her that I was black and that this was the real concern. I always thought it was Bob's best friend, Steve, who made that call. I never really felt that he was ok with the race situation. Bob's mother confronted him with the information she had received and demanded our phone number. His mother contacted my mother and decided that they should talk about their children. The call went like this:

"Hello, I am Mrs. Richards, Bob's mother. Am I speaking with Leticia's mother?"

"Yes you are," my mom responded.

Mrs. Richards said, "I think there is a problem that we should talk about."

"I agree. You are welcome to come here," my mom said.

They made arrangements to meet. Apparently, it never occurred to Bob's mom that I was black. Bob didn't tell her either.

When the doorbell rang, I hid out of sight but close enough to hear what was going on. Our mothers got off to a pretty bad start. My mom answered the door.

"I am here to speak with the lady of the house," Bob's mom announced.

"I am the lady of the house," Mom huffed back. "You must be Bob's mother." I wished I had a camera. Mrs. Richards was horrified.

I can see how she could have thought my mom was the maid. Bob and his family lived on the northeast side of town. They lived in a small row home in the middle of the block. The northeast side of town was not considered to be one of the nicest places to live. My family lived on the west side of town. We lived in a large single-family home that sat majestically on a green grassy bank. At the time, the neighborhood was considered upscale. Many of the people in the west end had people of color who worked for them as housekeepers or cleaning ladies, even maids.

Our mothers discussed and agreed that there would never be a marriage and that the relationship had to end. Bob's father was openly not a fan of blacks so he was left out of the discussion. Just like that, Bob was gone from my life. Although, we tried to secretly keep in touch with phone calls for a while.

When I became visibly pregnant, I stopped going to church. Bob told the teacher who led the church group that the baby was not his. That hurt beyond belief. *After all, he loved me, right?* I remember that we had a fight about him denying that he was the baby's father during which he called me a nigger. I never thought that would ever happen.

I had the baby, and now at the age of sixteen, I was a mother of two. Bob came to see the baby a few times.

One day I received a disturbing call from Bob. I knew even the calls would stop after what came next. "Someone wrote *nigger lover* all over my car," he said. "My father saw it and found out about you. And then he beat the shit out of me with a belt buckle."

After that there were messages through friends and two clandestine meetings. Then no contact at all. I heard later he was doing drugs and was arrested.

A few years later, just before I was to be married, Bob reached out to me. I met with him. He seemed tormented. He was scattered, and his movements were erratic at times. He kept talking about the way his life was turning out.

"All the bad things in my life are your fault," he yelled at me, and then took out a knife. I was sure I would die that night. However, he just kept playing with the knife, sometimes tauntingly while he spoke.

"Don't get married," he demanded.

He said he needed time to straighten out his life. He needed time to get a job and get off drugs. I was two weeks away from a big church wedding. It was clear that he needed help that I could not give him. I made the decision to stay on course and get married. I never expected to see Bob again. I ran into him years later at the fair with his wife and kids. It was a quick hello.

You Would Rather What

IN THE EARLY SEVENTIES WHILE IN HIGH SCHOOL, I DECIDED THAT I did not want a nun strum to be the extent of my guitar skills, so I found a guitar teacher and started lessons. Peter arrived at my front door guitar in hand. We became fast friends, bonding through music. I was in awe of Peter. He was my music man. Peter was a skilled musician and performer. He often played his guitar and sang for me. On occasion, I would join in, and we would instinctively vacillate between melody and harmony.

Strikingly handsome with blonde hair and blue eyes, he sported a kind of hippie persona that I found captivating. He was sort of a love child, circa 1960. He even had a Volkswagen. We spent a lot of time together, which led to us performing together, which led to us spending more time together. I developed quite a crush on him. It was not mutual. One day while we were rehearsing, I got caught up in the music and the moment.

"I value our time together, Peter, and I love making music with you. I would like to have more with you. I think I love you, and … well say something. What do you think?"

He replied without skipping a beat, "I would rather shoot myself in the head." He was as serious as a heart attack. His face void of expression. His body tensed up. His reaction was so visceral that it just made me feel worse because, now I felt repulsive, at least to this person that I loved.

Not exactly the response I was looking for, even in a letdown. There was an awkward silence, then laughter. Yes, we both laughed. My heart was bleeding. I didn't let it show. My response to his comment was, "Okay then, what song shall we work on next? You pull the tune. I will get us something to drink," I said.

We never spoke of it and continued to perform together for some time after that. I took the risk. The important thing is that it didn't stop me from taking the risk again.

A few years later, when I realized that I was a *fag hag* and had been for some time, it occurred to me that Peter, my soft-spoken, gentle, flower-child may have been gay. I thought he was just being a gentleman. But, I did learn later that being gay and dating women are not mutually exclusive.

Part III

Marriage: The First Go Round

I WAS VERY HAPPY TO GRADUATE AND MOVE ON. I MARRIED MY high school boyfriend, James, two weeks after graduation. It only made sense. We were the only two black kids in the group. We were friends. People were always trying to hook us up. Actually, I was dating Dale, the best friend of my husband-to-be. The problem was that my boyfriend was also dating anyone, and everyone, else.

One day a huge fight ensued between me and Dale that involved a thrown typewriter, among other things. James explained what an ass his best friend was and helped me through the hurt and humiliation. I don't need that "fuck snoot," I ranted and carried on completely unaware that my friend James had feelings for me.

"I can do the same as my ex," I declared. "The next guy that asks me to go out, I am his."

"Will you be my girl?" James asked.

Wow. Well, I said it, and he held me to it.

It was weird at first, but soon the idea of being his steady grew on me. We had been close friends, so we just kicked it up a notch. It made sense at the time. Our friends were both relieved and happy.

A year and a half later during a football game, he proposed. I was a pom-pom girl. He would come to all my games and sit on the riser behind me. One Friday night, I jumped up to cheer. He pushed me down in my seat, pulled out a ring and said, "Will you marry me?" I said yes, and that was that.

We moved into a large apartment directly across the street from my mom's house. It was just right for my two kids and us and close enough to mom who would babysit.

However, things did not go as I planned, and the kids stayed at my mom's house. I couldn't believe that my mother was literally stealing my children, refusing to let me take them with me, threatening legal action to get custody. She told me that she would be a better mother and that I was not equipped to be a mother. How would she or anyone know this? I rarely got the chance to function in that capacity. Worse, she had others in the family telling me what an awful person I was to hurt her by trying to take them with me. No one seemed to care how I felt, especially not my mother. She saw them as her children.

As the kids got older, I found out that she told them that I left them with her because my career was more important to me, I didn't care about them, I didn't love them or want them and other negative things that would impact my relationship with each of my kids depending on what she said to which child. Even though I was always a part of their lives, we had separate addresses. This kind of relationship sabotage and other negative subliminal messages colored my relationships with my kids and was difficult for the children to navigate. It is still difficult for me to understand. This was all a total departure from who I knew my loving mother to be.

As I was constantly reminded, they were just across the street. I did see them every day but it wasn't the same as living in the same space. Now I really understood why she got so angry with me when I made it clear to the kids that I was their mother. I remembered that she let people think that my oldest was my brother for a while. I did not go along with that for very long. This was way too much to for me to absorb at thirteen.

I started college six weeks after we married, while continuing to work full time. We had a child two years later.

It was tough juggling three kids, school, and a job. Even with mom watching the kids. Having kids when you are a kid presents a unique set of parenting issues between mother and grandmother.

The Super Jocks

THE SUMMER AFTER MY FIRST YEAR OF COLLEGE, I TOOK A JOB AT a local institution for the mentally ill. I worked in recreation at that time. I made some friends at work who later became friends outside the job. I spent a lot of time with Mitch through whom I met many other people. That group of friends later became affectionately known as the Super Jocks because they were very easy on the eyes.

I was in hog heaven because not only did I have a wonderful circle of friends, but also they were very handsome, talented guys, and they all seemed to love me, some more than others. We shared interests that I didn't share with my husband. We sang together and loved to sing show tunes. Most of us were in college or finished with school, and we worked at the same place. My husband and I worked opposite shifts, so he only hung out with us on occasion. Hanging out with us was not his favorite thing to do. I know he was happy about spending time with my friends in the same way working on cars, hard rock, and smoking dope was my idea of a good time. We were very different people.

Every weekend, the guys would come over for dinner, and we would hang out. Every weekend, like clockwork, they would leave between 10:30 and 11:00 p.m. I knew they were going somewhere after they left my apartment. I was hurt after a while that they never asked me to join them. I found out later that they often discussed wanting me to join them.

One Saturday night, the guys came for dinner as usual. We laughed and carried on much of the night. We were very campy at times. Everyone had a different name that usually had to do with their employment for example, there was Connie Cosmetology and Dolly Dugan to name a few. At one point, Andre emerged from my bathroom wearing my shower cap and waving my bath brush. Everyone laughed. He looked so silly. He then proceeded to go around the room dubbing each of our friends *fairies*. He approached each person, tapped them on the head and said, "Poof! You're a fairy." We all laughed so hard we couldn't talk.

Suddenly, all eyes were on me. I took the bath brush away from Andre and dubbed him a fairy. We all continued to entertain each other with songs and more jokes. We never needed to watch *Saturday Night Live*. We were *Saturday Night Live* every week.

Soon the clock struck ten, and things began to settle down. Someone said the words, "Have to go soon," followed by, "We are going out for a drink, do you want to come with us?" My head nearly exploded. Of course, I said yes! They waited for me to change. By 10:30, like always, they were off, but with one slight change, I wasn't left behind.

We drove downtown to a place that I knew I had passed a hundred times but never paid attention to. There was a big, brown, very plain door. As we entered, I was ushered past the bar to a booth-like table. I was instructed to slide in. My friends immediately surrounded me. It felt almost claustrophobic. Two people slid in next to me on either side. The other four sat across from me. Still caught up in the fact that my friends included me, it hadn't occurred to me that I didn't drink and had never tried it. I had no idea what to order. The guys decided I should try a daiquiri. The DJ was playing Donna Summer. I looked around the dimly lit room. There were a few people at the bar, and a few people dancing on the slightly elevated dance floor.

"What is this place called?" I asked. The table got noticeably quiet.

Someone quietly answered, The Stonewall. We were in Allentown, Pennsylvania. The name Stonewall meant nothing to me.

I responded, "It's nice, kind of quiet."

Just then, the waitress came to take our order. She was wearing a black and white tube top and denim cutoff shorts. She had a funky haircut, longer and curled on one side and beauty queen makeup. She took our drink order and seemed to know all my friends well. They introduced her to me. Her name was Georgette. When she left to get our drinks, I mentioned to the guys that I thought Georgette was the most flat-chested woman I had ever met. There was an awkward silence broken by an invitation to dance.

I quickly accepted as I love to dance. Donna Summer was singing, *try me try me try me.* I began to notice that there were several little groups dancing and a few couples that were men. As I danced and turned around, I began to suspect that I wasn't in Kansas anymore. Then I saw a familiar face from across the room at the bar. I saw two girls exchanging a kiss. One of them was familiar. It was the daughter of my mother's friend, Grace. With a flood of thoughts, it all became very clear to me.

I took off running from the dance floor followed immediately by my friends. I headed for the door. It was like a bad movie. I was running down the street toward a parking garage with several men running behind me yelling my name, telling me to stop. By then I was crying. I entered the parking garage and ran to the top. Someone yelled, "Don't jump!" I wasn't going to. I stopped because there was a half wall. I was at the top. It wasn't that big or high. Sometimes my friends were so dramatic. The obvious question followed.

"Why didn't you tell me?" I got a hug and an explanation.

"We were afraid that you wouldn't be our friend anymore."

In that moment, *Poof! You're a fairy,* had meaning. I questioned every kiss, every hug, and their fascination with breasts. We talked a bit more. They walked me to my car, and I went home. At least I now knew where they went when they left me. We remained friends, and I openly became their *fag hag,* a term of endearment.

My friends continued to come over on weekends and our bond was somehow stronger. I was happy about this since my social life mostly consisted of their visits. I didn't get out much. After a while my husband and I found that we had very little in common. He grew tired of hearing about my gay friends and Broadway shows and I had little interest in smoking weed with the guys, hard rock or cars. There were other issues. I made the very difficult decision to leave. I was pretty unhappy and tired. I dropped out of school. I moved in with a friend, one of the Super Jocks. My life changed dramatically. I started singing in clubs.

We went out dancing at the "Wall" every week, sometimes several times a week. On Sundays, we drove to New Jersey to the Musical Bar. I loved the Musical. It was a small neighborhood biker bar, but on Sundays, it transformed into a gay bar with often a mixed crowd, but mostly gay. There was a small dance floor and a jukebox that played favorites, old and new. Everyone was so nice, and we got to know people. The bartender was beyond cool. He was straight and treated everyone the same.

One Sunday afternoon, the guys stopped by to play Monopoly. I had planned to stay home when the game was over. The boys were ready to ride. Me? I was comfortable in my zip-front leopard housecoat and matching black fuzzy slippers. I was tired and happy to sit this one out. The guys just kept at me.

"I am not dressed and I shouldn't spend the money," I protested.

"Oh honey, you are dressed fine and fabulous!" they replied and off we went, fuzzy slippers and all.

I grabbed my purse and also a handful of Monopoly money. A funny joke, I thought. After all, I was dressed in loungewear. It was already funny.

We danced and had a few drinks. I went to the bar to buy another drink. This time I was joking with the bartender about buying drinks for everyone in the place. I showed him my Monopoly money, and he laughed.

"Drinks on Leticia, everyone!" he announced over the loudspeaker.

"You know I am paying you in Monopoly money, right!" I hollered over the music and cheers.

We were both laughing so hard.

"Yes, dear, I know," he said.

There were at least twenty-five people in the bar. I gave him my Monopoly money. He gave me a kiss on the cheek. That's what it was like for me at the bar with my friends. It was the 1970s. Disco was where the happy people went, and everyone loved everyone most of the time. I loved the seventies, and still do.

I sometimes miss my friends: Georgette, the guys, and my dear Veruska, a seven-foot drag queen who more than once helped me dress for the bar. He was so creative. Once, he took my wok, draped chiffon through the handles, and wore it as a hat. I remember how he and I stood at the door of the club and, as people entered, greeted each and everyone, saying, "Welcome to my party."

Oh, and we danced almost non-stop. I never was at a loss for a partner. Some of the guys and I actually had a dance routine to some of the more popular songs. But the girls, the real ones, could be catty. I walked off the dance floor one night and a woman approached me and said, "You dance pretty good for a fat girl." She was just jealous. Like many, she wanted to be in the sphere of the Super Jocks. Guys would make friends with me just to try to meet my friends. This made me very, very popular.

The Super Jocks and I were inseparable until AIDS hit, and people started to move away or leave us.

One night at a bar, I ran into a family friend, Doug, who was my babysitter when I was little, and his friend, Frenchie. I never asked how Frenchie got that name, but I discovered that I had really been a fag hag for a long time. It all seemed so odd to me that before age twenty-one I had no clue about gay people. When I got the education, I still thought that gays were in small pockets of my small little town in groups of two or three or in

New York City. My best friends were gay, and I was totally clueless for a long time. Color me stupid.

There were fringe people who were not part of the Super Jocks. They were friends that on occasion hung out with me and my friends. We all started going to a new club called The Library. The Library was a straight club. Hands down, the music, dancing, and fun were much better at the Wall. At 11:00 or so, we would leave and hit The Stonewall.

During this time, I met Ken.

Learning What Love Isn't

KEN HAD GONE TO THE SAME HIGH SCHOOL AS MITCH WHO WAS
often part of the group. We were all out for our usual night of cruising, dancing and prancing starting at The Library. Ken came along. Mitch invited him.
Oh, Ken was smooth. He asked me to dance. We danced all night. It was as
if the others were not in the room, let alone at our table.

We moved on as usual to the Stonewall for more fun, better music for
dancing, and more interesting people. I really had the time of my life at that
point. I felt like Cinderella rubbing elbows and other things with the prince.
He said all the right things and made all the right moves. He was tall, very
handsome and quite the fashion plate. He had a good job, believed in God,
drove a cool sports car, and sang. More importantly, he seemed to like me.
He was a soap opera leading man type. He was not at all the type of person
anyone, including me, would expect to see me with as a date.

The next day he showed up at my door with a flower and that killer
smile. When I opened the door, he started singing, *when will I see you again?*
When will we share precious moments? You know the song. I couldn't believe
it. Prince Charming was pursuing me, an over-weight black divorced mother
of three. This must be my something special. I think I fell for him right then
and there. After this day, we were an item. We spent so much time together
that even the Super Jocks were concerned.

The Miracle continued. He loved music and sang in a church choir.
He liked my kids. He was perfect for me. I loved to cook. He loved to eat.

We sang together. We danced. We were *The Young and the Restless* meets the *Bold and the Beautiful.* It wasn't long before we became more than an item. We were a couple.

I was so into him and the idea that someone like him could want me that I didn't notice for a long time that, when I drove, I had to drop him off a block from the house where he lived with his parents. I thought it was cool that we went out of town to dinner. When we went out during the day, it was always a romantic outing to a secluded park or a walk in the woods. Instead of going to a local pool or beach area, we went to a creek in the park by old railroad tracks. While it is a bit icky, wading in a creek with Prince Charming and a bar Ivory Soap—yes it does float—seemed romantic at the time. He had a degree in forestry. I thought he just loved the outdoors. It did give me cause for pause when he chased me through the woods trying to pee on me. There is something about a urinating penis coming at you that makes you run. Lucky for me, he finished before he caught up to me. I thought, *kinda playful in a porno flick kind of way.*

When we started talking about marriage, I nearly lost my mind. I was so happy. While I had spoken to his mom many times on the phone, and she was wonderful to me, we had not met. We had been dating for three years, and I had not met his family. My family loved Ken. He told me that the fact that I was not a Catholic would be an issue. *Really, that is the big issue?* I contacted his church and began to take classes with the nuns.

Things didn't change when he bought a house and moved from his parents' home. The fact that he preferred that I use the back door when I visited didn't matter or seem odd to me at the time. *The things you do for love.* I was so dutiful that I scared myself. I loved helping him out with things around the house like dishes, laundry, general clean up. I didn't even get angry when he unfolded some of the laundry I had just folded.

"You don't do it right," he said, and would proceed to teach me his proper way. *Really?*

If I was going to marry Snapper from *The Young and the Restless*, I could handle a little Felix Unger. Besides there wasn't a thing he could do to kill my passion, my undying love for him. Believe me, if eating watermelon over my naked body didn't send me running, nothing would. Mrs. Chancellor always said, "Pride is an emotion that a woman in love cannot afford." Don't you just love the soaps?

It took a very, very long while, but after many disappointments, bizarre treatment, two other women, and three men, I needed to reevaluate the concept of love versus stupidity. *What would Katherine Chancellor do?*

I sucked it up and threw him a birthday party. I wanted it to be a surprise party at a local restaurant. The party was shaping up to be as grand and as wonderful as I pretended he was. I was making a guest list when I realized that we had been together several years, but I still didn't know any of his friends or family outside of the guys in my circle.

Later that day, I was at his house taking down the laundry that was hanging out back. The next-door neighbor was outside, and we struck up a conversation about how doing laundry is a drag, blah blah blah. She was very friendly. I finished tidying up and the laundry. I left as always, the way I came in, out the back door. I hid the key where Ken kept it, and off I went.

A few blocks away, I had an idea. Ken had spoken about how nice his neighbors, Kelly and Joe were, and, yes, Kelly and I had had a lovely chat earlier.

"They will be my neighbors one day," I said out loud with a grin. "Why not invite them to the party?"

I turned around and headed back to Ken's neighborhood. I parked out front because I planned to go see the neighbors. It actually felt weird to be there because I had only been in the front of the house two or three times. I knocked on the door and was greeted with two warm smiles.

"What's up?" Joe asked.

"I'm throwing Ken a surprise party," I said, "and want you come."

"Why, thank you," Kelly said. Then she and Joe exchanged a glance that caught my attention, but didn't really mean much at the time. "Of course we'll be there."

I was thrilled! Now this really would be a surprise. Ken would never expect Kelly and Joe.

"Really nice to meet you," Joe said as he reached out to shake my hand. "What a nice person you are to give your boss a surprise party. I have never heard of a maid doing that."

I smiled and quickly turned, so that they couldn't see my tears or my head explode. *He tells people I am his maid! What do I do now? What would Mrs. Chancellor do?* She would throw a fierce and spare-no-expense party.

I stayed away from Ken all week, which seemed to be fine with him. On Saturday, we left to meet our usual mutual group of friends for a bite to eat before going to the disco, or so he thought. He entered the room, and everyone yelled, "Surprise!" As he got closer to the table, he saw his next-door neighbors. I planted a great big kiss on his lips and hung on his arm. He was horrified. His neighbors were puzzled. He hardly spoke during dinner, and it was clear that dancing was off the table. We fought all the way to his house. I dropped him off out front. He didn't call or answer my calls for two weeks.

In the interim, Kelly told me about the blonde who came to the house often when I wasn't around. Kelly told me that she was introduced to her as Ken's girlfriend, Susan.

He finally called me. He wanted to talk. I was beyond crushed, but still glad he wanted to come over. I tried to be a hard ass and confront him.

"Susan goes to my church and is just a friend that my mother wants me to be with. I dated her for my mother," Ken explained as if he were the victim. "My mother won't approve of you because you aren't Catholic."

He always could play me like a baby grand. Before the hour was up, he was singing to me. Holding me tightly in his arms, he swore, "Baby, I promise to straighten up, fly right and love you forever."

He knew just where and how to touch me both physically and emotionally. His long index finger softly moved my hair away from my face. He held my face in both his hands, while he used his thumbs to wipe away my tears. He slowly brought my face to his, kissing me ever so gently on the lips.

A few weeks later, we were out with the gang for our usual dancing and prancing at The Wall. The guys were unusually tacky this night, outright mean. I knew they thought Ken and I were a bad idea. I heard all of their arguments many times. However, on this night the cracks and comments were not private and were relentless as if they were trying to make us, well Ken more than me, uncomfortable. There was a guy at the bar who was clearly cruising Ken, and everyone noticed. Sure, the guy was cruising Ken. He was hot eye candy. I was used to guys trippin', after all the Wall was a gay bar.

On this night though, the looks and comments were an issue, even for Ken. Before the night was over, I found myself siting outside on the dirty front steps of a bar, dressed in disco chic from head to toe, being asked the question every woman wants to hear from the man she loves. "Why does everyone think that I'm gay?" Followed by, "Do you think I'm gay?"

I couldn't breathe. I just wanted to dance and let the music take me anywhere else. Dance was what we came to the club to do. Disco was where the happy people went. My brain did not want to have this conversation. Was there really an answer to this question that would get us back on the dance floor? No, there wasn't.

"It really only matters what you think," I said to him. "I don't care what people say. Talk is cheap. If you tell me you are gay, that's something different. I have to believe it. But I wouldn't care if you were. I love you."

The embrace we had during this conversation was interrupted by his tears. I found myself quietly stroking his hair as his head pressed deeply against my heart, and he sobbed. In that moment, the only pain I could feel was his.

"Ken, it's ok. Are you trying to tell me something?"

"I love you," he said. This may have been the most authentic moment of the entire relationship.

We never again spoke of that night, ever.

The bar was a fun place for dancing and a few laughs, but it could be brutal. I wasn't much of a drinker, but I would dance the night away. I was never at a loss for a dance partner. I loved dancing with Gary. It was like ballroom disco. I was Ginger, and he was Fred, or vice versa. At one point, some people stopped dancing to watch us.

Queens can be so mean. There was another fag hag regular at the Wall. Perry was queen of the Wall disco diva until I arrived on the scene. She was not happy to share her position or lose her crown. One night some people at the bar were making fun of her looks. Perry had very bad acne and lots of pockmarks on her face. She always did makeup, but it didn't really hide anything. That night at the Wall, they actually took up a collection for her and told her to have her face sand blasted. Some people laughed. I didn't think it was funny. I could see the hurt on her face, even through tons of makeup. She continued to laugh with her so-called friends who started this hurtful joke, and took the bag of money that was collected and presented to her like an Academy Award. Yes, the DJ stopped the music for the presentation.

The Wall was a strangely terrifying place in a haunted house kind of way. You could live or die there. If you were young and good-looking, the Wall was your oyster. If you were average looking or over thirty, the Wall was not always so nice, and your expiration date made a difference between going home alone or hot sex. Fat or not, I never had that problem. I was queen of the fag hags.

I got a New Year's Eve gig with the band that I was a singer in. I was so excited! For me, this would be a huge party that didn't cost me money, I would get to sing, and the pay was to be excellent. The only drawback was not being able to spend New Year's Eve with Ken. The next week at rehearsal, the guys in the band told me that the person who booked us made it part of the deal for us to bring spouses or a friend or two. Problem solved. Spending New Years with my love, how romantic. I could sing to him all night.

My very best friend in the world was more than that. He was a twin brother from a Caucasian mother. Tim and I met when he signed on to help out at a benefit performance that I was doing for the March of Dimes. We became instant friends, spending hours together talking, sharing, dreaming, and talking more. I remember being on the phone at all hours with him for hours on end.

Once I had a dream that I bombed Ken's house. It was so real to me that I called Tim in the middle of the night and asked him to come with me to see if the house was still standing and Ken was ok. He would have deserved it. Cheating on me for his mother's sake with Susan, or as I liked to call her, Cantaloupe Woman. Ken was so taken with her gardening skills. He was always talking about his friend Susan's garden and how difficult it was to grow a cantaloupe. She grew two cantaloupes in her garden, and, "they were so delicious," he'd say. Anyway, my friendship with Tim was that close. He went with me to make sure I hadn't killed anyone. When we arrived at Ken's house, it was abundantly clear that I didn't bomb it. His car was parked out back as usual. The house was still standing, and there was a light on upstairs that could be seen from the outside.

One of our favorite things to do was to go Mickie D's and sit in the car eating french fries and drinking hot chocolate. It wasn't long before Tim and Ken met. I was already a friend of Tim's love interest, Jess. Jess and I met during a production of Finian's Rainbow. We were both cast members. More often than not, it was just Tim and I or the new group of guys he introduced me to. Those were fun times. Theater people are fun.

We often met at a section of a local park, at the parkway, a huge park made up of smaller parks. It was beautiful. You could park your car by the big rocks and walk into God's country. As far as you could see were shades of green. There were full, tall trees for shade if you wanted. On the right was an elevated woodsy area, lots more trees and some rocks. One time at night I went there with a friend for fun. Most people knew this place, the area of the park that we were in, as the gay part of the parkway, so we were safe. We took a bright flashlight with us. We thought it would be funny to shine the light into the cold darkness of the elevated woodsy area, so we did. Oh, the guys who scurried about were not happy. I think they thought we were the police. It was funny to see who ran out of those woods. We recognized some people one would never expect to see there and others who we did expect to see there.

On the right side, opposite the woods and back a ways was a path and sort of a bridge that led to a small island. There was a sparkling water stream that nature had decorated with rocks and tree branches that formed pools and waterfalls. Next to the stream was a massive willow tree. Our group of friends had claimed this island for our own. I would go there to think or be alone with nature. Sometimes I would take my guitar and sing, alone or with friends. Ken and I spent many romantic times at this park. My glasses were not rose colored. They were blood red.

My friend, Tim, had nothing to do for New Years. His other half was busy. It made perfect sense for my best friend, my brother, to join us for New Year's Eve; a free party where he would get to watch me perform and keep Ken company while I was working.

It was a typical New Year's Eve party with all the trimmings, very festive. I loved that a small crowd hung around the stage and was into the music, lots of dancing. On my breaks, I would join Ken and Tim at our table. They seemed to be having a good time. I saw them walking around and enjoying the evening.

Finally, it was time, almost midnight. The wives and girlfriends of the band made their way toward the stage. I didn't see Ken. There were still a few minutes before midnight. The band did the countdown, which was my cue to sing. Midnight came and all the wives and girlfriends came up to the stage for their New Year's kiss. I kept singing and scanning the crowd looking for Ken. This was an important moment for me, for us. A new year, a new beginning, starting off with a kiss, by his side, was, to me, a wonderful way to start the year.

Auld Lang Syne was now over, and still no Ken. Seeing the disappointment on my face, the guitarist said, "Ken probably went to the men's room or outside for a break. Go get your kiss."

The band covered for me while I went to find Ken and get my kiss. Imagine my surprise to find Ken out by my car giving my kiss—and more—to Tim. *Well, this sucks! My love and my brother on New Year's Eve. Now I have to go sing. Did I say this sucks? Turn around, go to the bathroom, pull yourself together and finish the set. There is no one I can talk to, nothing I can say to the band about what took me so long.* They joked, as bands often do, that must have been some kiss, cue drums and laughter. I was numb.

We finished the set and packed up. Ugh, the ride home. I drove us there in my car. I had questions, lots of them. I didn't want to talk. The ride home was quiet except for a few feeble attempts at conversation that I did not participate in. Most of the time Ken just kept looking straight ahead. In my mirror I could see Tim sitting quietly with his head down. I just kept wondering, how many times? How long had it been going on? What happened? Still numb.

The next day I realized I was over the top angry with Tim. I reasoned that Ken hurting me was expected; he did it often. I expected this behavior from the man I agreed to marry, not from the person I loved as my brother. I was so hurt. I saw Tim once or twice after this. Talking it out would not fix it. Nothing could. For years, I carried this hurt. It still amazes me that Ken and I got past this.

Yes, Ken and I actually survived this. There was groveling involved, promises and apologies. Time and music really can patch a broken heart. The problem is it never fully heals. It often bleeds through the patch. Anything at any time can cause the wound to hemorrhage.

We had to deal with the possibility—ok probability—that Ken was gay and how this would impact our relationship. Neither one of us wanted to break up at this point. I was so in love, or so I thought. It is awful to be in a relationship and still be alone. We agreed that he could see men on the side as long as it did not interfere with our life together. I didn't want to see it or know about it. That was the agreement.

Spring was now in the air. The flowers were blooming. The days were longer. Ken and I were good. Easter was around the corner. I called Ken on the phone. His mother answered and recognized my voice.

She was very pleasant. "Leticia, how are you, dear?" she asked.

I responded, "Fine thank you, and how are you?"

We chatted about the weather and the coming of spring. I talked about the special music for Easter that was keeping me busy. She commented that we had never met, although we had spoken many times. Out of the blue, she invited me to Easter dinner. How sweet. Of course, I accepted. When Ken got on the phone, he was actually okay with it. I was in the process of converting to Catholicism, so why not? I was so excited. I sent her a beautiful and expensive arrangement of flowers.

As I drove by the house later that week, I saw them proudly displayed in the large front window of their home. Could I be any happier? I was about to meet and have dinner with my future-in-laws. Could I ask for a better Easter? The plan was to go to Easter service together, and then go back to his parents' place for dinner. Since Ken's parents lived near the church, we planned to meet at the church.

I had to park two blocks away from the church, St. Joseph's Slavic Catholic Church. It was crazy congested and busy. As I approached the church steps, I saw Ken standing with his parents. I walked over to them. Ken said hello, then introduced me. His father was quiet without expression. His mother, her face Easter egg red, was clearly unhappy. We entered the church.

His parents refused to sit with us. They separated from us and sat toward the front of the church. I wasn't feeling the same Christian love that Ken's mother had offered on the phone. Ken and I sat in the back of the church. When the service was over, we walked outside and waited for his parents to catch up. His parents followed the crowd up the aisle, into the vestibule and out the large wooden doors.

His mother walked over to us and exploded, "You brought this nigger here?"

I felt like the lead story on the six o'clock news. If any of the other people didn't notice the spot of color in the church before, they did now. There were many people standing in front of the church and many more still exiting the building. When she uttered the word *Nigger*, every head turned and looked at me. *Really, on the front steps of a church that you just prayed in and listened to the Easter homily in?*

She said her piece, screamed her piece. "Nigger, you will never marry my son. You have embarrassed and deceived us." she said.

Soon she just became a big head yelling at me. I couldn't speak. Ken didn't try to speak up for me or us. He and his parents left me in shock in front of the church. Churchgoers were driving by slowly and staring at me.

As they left, the priest approached me. "I'm sorry," he said, "but you don't fit in. We don't want your kind here." He recommended that I go to the inner-city parish not far away where there would be "more of my kind".

I was beyond humiliated and outraged at the same time. *Bigotry in the name of God? On Easter Sunday?* There was no empathy or compassion for me. I was less than a person. I was a thing, a kind of thing. He gave me directions to Immaculate Conception Church; it was an Irish Catholic church. I couldn't speak. I knew if I opened my mouth to say one word, I would cry. I found my way to the car.

On the way home, I passed Ken's parents' house. I saw the flowers that I had sent were gone from the window. As I drove by, I could see that they were sitting in the garbage can. I could not process. *What happened? I went to God's house on Easter Sunday, and I wasn't welcome there. What? Ken's mom lost her bigoted mind. What? Guess who's coming to dinner?* He never told his bigoted parents that I was a woman of color, not that it should matter.

Ken came to my house. I opened the door and said, "You left me standing there alone."

"I went with my folks to try to reason with mother who was very upset," he explained. "I didn't tell them you are black because it doesn't matter."

"Why didn't you warn me that they didn't know?" I asked.

No response from Ken.

"Clearly it does matter. It has always mattered. Why do we never go out in public alone? We are always with the group or out of town. It matters! It matters to your parents and to you Ken." I argued.

"This will change," Ken promised. This would change, indeed. He would change.

We made plans to go to Ohio to visit my aunt. I had never been on a plane. Ken was going along to hold my hand. I thought, this is great, we need a vacation together, just the two of us. I bought the plane tickets. We were all set to go.

I went alone. He backed out at the last minute. Why? A guy of course. He simply made other plans with his guy on the side. I was crushed with overwhelming feelings of hurt, anger, and humiliation. He had agreed that any guy on the side would never interfere with us. I had to face the facts. This was five years of crazy break-ups and make-ups. Nothing is worse than realizing that the love you lost, you never had.

Still, we both hung on. I don't know why or to what. I was starting to think, if Ken is a gift, God didn't send him. The wounds were hemorrhaging.

I felt physically ill for days. My heart hurt. I felt physical pain in my chest. A broken heart, perhaps? I was sitting alone at home contemplating life and death, my life or death, when a familiar numbness set in. I began crying. I couldn't stop. I got down on my hands and knees and prayed. I prayed hard:

"God, send me someone who will truly love me, and whom I can love, if not please take me. I can't bear this pain any longer. I can't pretend anymore." A thousand songs flooded my brain at once. Music is my safe place, even if the songs are sad.

You can't tell me that God isn't real! Two days later. I met Donna.

Learning What Love Is

I AGREED TO TAKE A PART-TIME JOB THAT I WAS MORE THAN QUAL-
ified for with a local Human Services Agency, with the agreement that in a few
months when the manager left, I would replace her. I would have full benefits
and a salary increase. When I reported for work one morning, I found a note
telling me to stop by the office later in the day. Of course, I knew why, it was
the manager's last day. There would be paperwork from personnel, and I fig-
ured some additional information they would give me.

When I arrived, the mood in the office was different, less relaxed, and
more formal. I was invited into an office where I was greeted by the woman
who hired me and her assistant. There was a large desk piled high with folders
and papers. The bay window behind the desk had no curtains at the top, letting in every ray of sunshine there was to be had. The two women sat oddly
close to each other and across the room from me. Usually, we sat in a circle
when we had meetings, even small ones.

Michelle, the woman who hired me spoke, first. "Tish, I will get right
to the point. We have hired staff for your building," she said.

"Wonderful!" I replied. "We are down two people and, as you know,
it has increased overtime. As a new manager, I would rather not inherit that
problem."

The next statement I did not see coming. "Well, we hired a manager
for your building." She jumped up. "Before you respond, let me say that you

are an exemplary employee. Your work has not gone unnoticed. Things are definitely better in your building since you have been there. We are certain that we will pass state inspection largely because of your work."

"I saw what needed to be done, and the state inspection would take place on what I thought was my watch," I interrupted. "If I am such a valuable employee, why are you giving the job you agreed to give me to someone else? I imagine that you hired off the street?"

Michelle's sidekick flinched but never made a sound. She sat legs crossed and arms folded almost like a hug the whole time.

"We have to follow company policy and hire a person with a degree. You have some college and a lot of experience. However, we must follow policy. She starts tomorrow. Your new assignment, in addition to your current duties, will be to train her."

I thought my head would explode. It was immediately clear to me why the office mood felt weird. It was their fear. They expected a huge angry explosion. *Sorry to disappoint. I was not raised that way.*

I had read the policies and procedures book. I never saw this rule. However, I later did some further checking. The person that I would have replaced did not have a degree. I had years more experience than she did. I also chatted up other managers to learn that only two out of five had degrees. All of them were white. So I got a lawyer.

In the meantime, the new manager arrived at the worksite. Donna was dressed in business attire and carried a very cool leather purse. She was fresh out of school with a degree in industrial psychology, but no experience in the job she was just hired to do, which was to manage staff and patients in a supervised group living facility for dual diagnosed patients. The company didn't even have the sense of responsibility to bring her to the job site and introduce her to the staff. She cautiously introduced herself to me. I was the only staff person in the office and on duty at the time.

"Hello," I said and immediately addressed the elephant in the room. "I am sure you are expecting me to be difficult and hard to work with. Please understand that my beef is with the company not you."

"They did tell me that you would give me a hard time," she responded, "and advised me to report everything to them, and they would handle it. They told me that you thought that you were getting the manager position and that you do not want to train me."

I explained what the real deal was and assured her that I would not give her a hard time or sabotage her in any way. I showed her around and then we talked about the company, her work experience, school and other small talk. By late afternoon, the daily work was finished. We discussed the fact that she was not from the area and didn't know many people, so I invited her to join my roommate and me for dinner.

Donna followed me home where we had dinner and more conversation. She really was a nice person. I couldn't have been mean to her even if they paid me. My roommate, John, liked her also.

That evening, we bonded over man troubles. She had been engaged and had caught her fiancée with another woman. Well, and me, I had Ken. After that evening, it was clear that there would not be any awkwardness at work, and we were well on our way to becoming friends.

The following week the weather was sheer torture. It was so hot. The building we worked in was not air-conditioned. My plan was to get finished and hit the pool where I lived immediately after work. Donna was coming to dinner again, so I invited her to come early to swim. I was informed by the office, that Donna had worked as a lifeguard. I loved the water but couldn't swim. We had a great time. I felt safe.

On the weekend, we went shopping and took in a movie. I had lots of friends, but most of my friends, especially the close ones, were gay men. It was nice to talk to a woman about things, especially about Ken. There was no judgment or put-downs when I was reduced to tears.

A few weeks later, Donna came over for dinner as she had several times before. After dinner, we listened to music and talked for a while, a long while. Then a kiss. I think we were both surprised. I know I was. Neither one of us had much experience in this area. Donna went home and left me to ponder the events of the evening. I was sure work would be weird. It wasn't. Nothing changed.

Donna and I went out to dinner on the weekend. I unloaded about Ken as usual. Donna's response was quick and to the point.

"Why do you stay with such an asshole?"

I sensed that she was frustrated. I was taken back by her tone. Usually she smiled, took my hand and was supportive.

Then she looked me in the eye and said, "Listen, if you want to continue to see me, you have to get rid of him."

What? I am calculating now, I have known her a month, kind of demanding. I get it; she is tired of drying my tears and hearing about Ken. Maybe she likes me. My mind continues to race. I was seeing Donna. No, really seeing Donna. I was dating a woman. My deliberation over the issue was quick. I reasoned; *Donna treats me like gold, Ken treats me like trash. Man, woman, does it really matter? Why not see what happens?* She did like me. I liked her. It wasn't a gay straight issue. It was who was the better person.

The verdict was in as fast as a commercial break on Judge Judy.

"Okay," I said, "okay."

I was uncertain about everything but relieved at the same time. That very day Ken and I were supposed to go watch my youngest play soccer. I looked at Donna, walked to the phone and called Ken.

"Ken, you are off the hook. Donna is going with me to the soccer game today." I heard a sigh of relief in his voice. *Jackass,* I thought to myself. "I will call you tomorrow."

"Phone breakups are so tacky and impersonal. I will call and go over there tomorrow," I told Donna. She giggled took my hands in hers and smiled. Just like that, Donna and I were a couple, off to the soccer game.

The next day, I called Ken and went to his house to break the news. When I arrived, Ken was making cream of mushroom soup from scratch. Of course he was, and with mushrooms Susan grew in her very own mushroom garden next to her cantaloupe. Steamy warmth filled the room, making the house even cozier. We sat at the kitchen table as we often did. I saw no reason to beat around the bush.

"Ken, there is no easy way to say this. You have got to know that our relationship has been in trouble for years."

He took my hand in his and said, "It's had its ups and downs. But, we are doing much better now."

"Better for who?" I asked.

He went on to talk about all the fun we had together, and then he started to sing, *You are the one who makes me happy when everything else is grey. We were Jane Oliver fans. Really! Now we are dancing around the kitchen and into the living room.*

"Ken, I am trying to have a serious conversation with you."

He kept singing.

"I am breaking up with you," I said loudly.

"Come on, what's wrong?" he smiled and said. "Just give me a little time. I will straighten up and fly right. We're good. Come on, I love you."

"I am leaving you for Donna," I blurted out.

"Now I know this is a joke," he laughed.

My confusion quickly turned to anger. I grabbed my keys, headed for the door and said, "I just thought it was better to tell you in person."

"Wait!" he called out.

But I left. I had been waiting for her all my life.

In the weeks following, there were phone calls and unannounced visits from Ken. We even tried the friend thing. However, every time Donna left the room, Ken would try to hug me or grope me. He seemed to think that if he could just kiss me or get me interested in sex with him, I'd come back to him. You know many men think that, every woman needs a man or a dick. Ken didn't really want me. It was the challenge, the fact that I left him for a woman. After all, in the world according to Ken, what does that say about him?

Donna and I spent every free moment that we had together. Once Ken was out of the picture, I wondered why I waited so long. Donna treated me with dignity and respect. Wow, what a concept. I remembered being in the pool with her and feeling safe. Never really felt like that. She was a lifesaver in more ways than one. She was my lifesaver. Thank you, God!

One night, she invited me over to her place for dinner, which was big gesture because she didn't cook very much. Her one specialty was shrimp scampi. She presented me with a scrumptious meal complete with pasta, a tossed salad and bread. Donna was so proud of herself, she was beaming. We had salad and bread, then I had to break the news to her that I couldn't eat the shrimp. She was very understanding, but clearly disappointed. I was fine. I was just happy to be with her. We were relaxed, no pretense. We kissed and the night turned into morning. It was clear that our friendship had an added dimension of romance, maybe love. This significant day became our anniversary.

Terror struck the next day. *What am I doing? I have kids and a mom. I go to church.* Then I looked at Donna, and it just felt right. Donna had a luminous smile and a heart of gold. She had a calming effect on me. I loved her swimmer shoulders and back. I loved the way she took my hand or arm when we were out at a gay club or at a friend's house. She made me feel like eye candy, but she was the eye candy. It seemed as if Donna held everything that I said, thought or did in her heart and hands. Everything from me was important to her.

When we had a chance to move in together, we took it. I owned a house that was being rented, but the tenants hadn't paid rent in six months. When the house became vacant, we decided to get some work done on it and moved into the house together. More romance. We slept on the floor because we didn't have furniture our first week there. Meals were take-out food, picnic style in the center of the living room on the floor. We spent a lot of time looking for furniture, fixing up the house, and making it a home.

Three months later the agency we worked for settled the discrimination lawsuit that I had engaged a lawyer to file against them. Donna and I both moved on to jobs at another agency, the same agency. We were ecstatic about both outcomes.

Donna and I were, and continue to be, joined at the hip. We lived together, commuted and, for a time, worked together, and spent our free time together. We just got along so well. It actually bothered some of our friends, and they spoke freely about it. Some even tried to come between us. In the end, nothing ever worked. *What God has joined together . . .*

We lived in a German Catholic, inner-city neighborhood. Our home was a five- bedroom row house. It had a nice size front porch with a huge front window, above which was a beautiful rectangular piece of stained glass that ran the width of the window. When you entered the home, there was a small vestibule with a door made of cut glass and wood that led to a twenty-nine-foot living room. It was a very spacious home with lots of character.

Next door, on either side, lived two older women, sisters, Aggie and Marie. They were very Catholic and of German heritage. Marie was tall with fiery dark eyes and dark hair. Aggie was a bit shorter than her sister with the same eyes and hair. She was not as feisty as Marie. Both women had the same weekly beauty parlor hair do. They were polite and occasionally sweet, but mostly they were the nosy neighborhood gossips. Summer, winter, spring and fall, you could hear them having full conversations outside. Our backyard was between them, but that didn't stop them from talking about us. They just spoke loudly across the two fences. I wonder now why they didn't just use the phone to gossip. I often heard the neighborhood news from them. My office was upstairs in the back of our home. If the window was open, I always got an ear full.

I have always been very social, and that didn't change when Donna and I got together. There were always people at our house for dinner, a party, or just to hang. It never occurred to me that after high school I didn't have many friends that were girls or women. But evidently, the sisters noticed.

One bright, sunny, cheery day, I opened the window in my office that overlooked the backyard. Both women had hung their laundry to dry in the sweet fresh summer breeze. I love that song! *Summer Breeze*. I could also see and hear our lovely neighbors gossiping as usual, each woman standing at the center of their yards near the middle of their fences.

Marie started, "Did you hear that music last night? Disgusting!"

"I can't believe they were in the yard," Aggie, not to be outdone, added fuel to the fire. "I am sure they had wine out there also."

"It's bad enough that they parade all their men in and out of the house, but an open outside party with their customers is too much," catty Marie went on. "Can't believe that the cops haven't raided the place yet. Whores living and working right next door!"

Outraged, Aggie shot back, "I told you the neighborhood would go to pot. Mamie across the street told me that she saw Sadie's boy go in there just last week."

It was very clear that the two women thought that Donna and I were hookers, and all of our gay male friends were johns. This would have been hysterically funny had there not been the realization that other neighbors, too, thought that Donna and I were running the neighborhood brothel. I had heard enough.

I went downstairs and out back to greet the ladies. "Good morning, how's it going?"

Both women smiled, with an I got caught with my hands where they don't belong kind of smile. Clearly Aggie wanted to crawl under a rock, Marie not so much.

"Fine, how are you? Quite a gathering you had last night," one of them replied.

"Oh yes," I said. "We had lots of fun. We always do when our friends visit. You know, we are having a cookout on Saturday, why don't you come over?"

I thought both women would pass out. They quickly made excuses and ran in the house.

When Saturday rolled around, I was out in the yard setting up when Marie called to me from her porch. She met me at the fence and gave me a bowl of freshly made German potato salad. "I noticed how you could use a little help with your potato salad, so I made some for the cookout."

I was completely surprised by the salad but even more deeply concerned how she knew anything about my potato salad, which is very good still. I was also surprised that she planned to join us. She went on to explain the difference between our salads, bacon for one, then back inside she went.

As it turned out, Marie only sort of joined us. She stayed in her yard during the picnic. I gave her food over the fence. It was funny, like she thought she would catch something or be labeled a hooker. She sat outside most of the evening taking it all in, occasionally talking over the fence. Aggie was a no-show but could occasionally be seen peering out the upstairs window. Funny, after that day, both women were friendlier, and I heard no more talk about the whores next door. They even tried to include me in their gossip sessions. Sometimes, people just want to be included.

Our friend, Gus, came to live with us at the request of his father. It seems that Gus, who was a senior in high school at the time, had managed over the years to get kicked out of several schools. This time, his father was able to get him into the only Catholic high school that just happened to be a few blocks down the street from us in our German Catholic neighborhood.

Gus was a very sweet guy trying to find his way in the world, just like the rest of us. Gus lit up any room he entered. He had a sugary childlike spirit that matched his bright eyes and stylish hair. He was a teddy bear. Gus was a class act and a lot of fun. I still have a picture of him wearing my wedding gown, holding a dildo for a bridal bouquet and another where he wore a party hat with one of my sparkly tops draped over his shoulder.

He had lost his mother at an early age and had a father and brothers who just didn't quite get the gay thing. So there were issues, and Donna and I were glad to help. Coming from a family with means, Gus' father took care of his expenses, including rent. Even before Gus moved in with us, he always seemed to have just about anything he wanted. In high school, if you have a nice car, cash and credit cards in your pocket, that is everything. Gus was kind, thoughtful and generous.

I had a weekly gig at the Civic Center Hilton in Philadelphia. One evening as I was getting ready to leave, there was a knock at the front door. It was a deliveryman with a brilliantly red bouquet of roses adorned with baby's breath. Donna put them in water for me as I hurried to gather my things. The card said, "You should be treated like the star that you are." Gus was also a bit flamboyant, and was used to the finer things in life. I was not.

At that moment, there was another knock on the door. *Really? We had to get to Philadelphia.* It was a man in a dark suit with a hat that looked as though he was an officer in the Navy. As I opened the door, I saw a long black car double parked and the neighbors across the street out on their porches.

"Can I help you?" I asked the man.

"I am here to pick up Ms. Walker and her companion," he replied, handing me a note that repeated the note that came with the roses that was signed, Love Gus.

Yes, Gus sent a limo to drive Donna and me to my gig in Philadelphia. Speechless and running late, we quickly got in the limousine and were off. The limo waited for us, and then took us home after my show. What a wild night.

There is an old saying, *you never know someone until you live with them.* I found this to be true. Gus moved in a few weeks into the school term. Gus' father trusted us to look after Gus, see that he got to school and things like that, even though we were not much older than Gus. We had not considered how our relationship might change some with the added dimension of substitute parenting. It did. We soon found that Gus had a few demons, had trouble getting to school, even two blocks away, and he drank; no, he was an alcoholic and all that it entails.

Donna and I tried talking to him and reasoning with him, but he would just say what he thought we wanted to hear. It wasn't long before he had spiraled out of control. He invented elaborate stories worthy of a soap opera to cover his tracks. To explain his absence from the house and late nights, he led us to believe that he was dating a wealthy man from Delaware. Once he had another friend of his call us pretending to be connected to this man in order to make his story more plausible. I even received flowers from this man that I had never met.

Gus came home one night very drunk. It was a school night, but he had every intention of going back out. Being the mom that I was, I said, "No way." We had words, and then I took his car keys. He was so drunk and angry that he grabbed the house phone from the end table and raised it to hit me in the head from behind. Luckily, another friend, Susan, that was staying with us happened to walk in the room and grabbed his arm just before the phone connected with my skull. Susan was tall, much taller than Gus. Just then Donna came in and screamed, "Gus!" He went to his room.

The next day, he was very apologetic. I think he realized that his elaborate drama was falling apart because we were now asking questions. Things didn't add up. Donna and I talked it out and made a plan. Our friend needed more help then we could give him, and he definitely needed specialized help. I made some calls and set it in motion. I called his father and advised him of what happened, and what we were going to do. He was immediately on board, gave us the information we needed to execute the plan, and thanked us for all we had done and tried to do for his son.

A few days later, after things settled down, I suggested that we go out to lunch, as we often did. Donna and I got in the car.

Gus got in the backseat. "Where are we going?" he asked.

"Not sure. Let's drive and see what looks good."

We were laughing and talking. Gus entertained us with stories about his dates and what not. He didn't even realize how long we had been driving, nearly an hour and a half.

When the car stopped, he commented that it didn't look much like a restaurant. Well, it could have been. It was a big very impressive manor type structure. It had a big and inviting wrap-around porch with a sign that said, Chit Chat Farms. The sign spoke of conversation and fresh food, so it worked. We went inside with him and walked to the front desk.

When they greeted him by name, he knew. He was a bit angry but agreed to talk with the counselor. He didn't panic because he understood how much he needed help.

But the issue came as we were leaving. He yelled to us, "I can't believe you are doing this to me. I can't believe you are leaving me here. You tricked me. I thought you were my friends. I sent you flowers."

Donna and I hurried to the car. We were both crying. We tried to console each other during the ride home. We just kept saying, "We left him there. It is what he needs, right?"

My head was spinning with second guesses. *We did the right thing, didn't we? It was only for thirty days. It is the best thing for him, the brochure said so. He hates us now for sure.*

Later, I heard he moved to a place in Minnesota for more treatment. We lost our friend until Facebook happened. Thirty years later, I received a beautiful letter from Gus thanking Donna and me for what we did. He has had many successes over the years. I am very proud and pleased to say he went back to school and is now a very successful drug and alcohol counselor. I love a happy ending, and we remain good friends

Yup, Donna and I do everything together. I love that about us.

I love being a mom much more than being a parent. Moms get to do all the cool, fun stuff that goes with having a kid, and kids always love Mom. *Mother* can be a wash between good and bad. But *parent,* that word, conjures up all kinds of things, mostly painful and always difficult. Being a parent means more than financial support, camping trips and days at the beach. Parents have to deal with it all, which includes discipline and saying "no" more often, unpleasant situations with teachers, and more.

I have to say that Donna and I did pretty well at parenting, considering our life experience with our own parents and the lack of a manual. I think being a kid, no matter your age, while raising a kid, is very helpful. I mean, staying in touch with your inner child. It makes understanding so much easier.

Things seemed to be falling in to place. There was only one thing missing. My kids, I wanted them to live with us, sleep at our house. Donna was so supportive and happy that this could happen for the kids and me. The boys were older and could be part of the decision. However, when asked, the boys chose to stay at my moms. It was hurtful but understandable. The boys continued to stay with my mom during the week so that they could stay in the same schools and be with their friends, an arrangement that I was never happy about. It seemed that the older the boys got, the more participation in school activities and the increased time spent with their friends, the less they came home to me and Donna on weekends or were available for outings. Sad for me but my inner child always keeps me in touch, so I get it. I took great comfort in knowing that if my kids needed me at any time, they would call, and they did. It made the living arrangement tolerable. Oh how I missed the days when they were little and would put on shows for mom and me, just like I had done as a child.

One night our oldest, Jayson, decided to come over. He needed to talk, as teenagers often do. It was late, and he didn't have his key. As he looked for a way to get into the house or to wake us, our very nosy neighbors called the police. Donna and I woke up to flashing red lights and police radio noises. We ran downstairs to look out the front window. To my surprise, we saw two cops on the front porch and one was physically holding Jayson with his arms pulled behind his back. We ran to the door. Aggie and Marie were outside along with several other neighbors.

The policeman said with a strange smirk on his face, "This guy says he lives here."

"He does, what is going on, and let him go," I said. "He is my son!"

The policeman dropped his grip, and Jayson came inside. Donna took him to the kitchen for some tea. The policemen apologized to me saying that they had received a call that there was a break-in at this address. They thought they had caught the guy when they got Jayson.

"Didn't he tell you who he was?" I asked. "He is a minor."

The cop laughed and responded, "Yes. These perps tell you anything."

"My son is *not* a perp, as you call him. You knocking on the door and asking us could have avoided all of this. Innocent until proven guilty, remember?"

Meanwhile, Aggie and Marie sheepishly slivered back into their houses. I was so angry. The next day, I filed a complaint with City Hall.

Shawn, our middle son, was always off on an adventure, with or without friends. Whether he was following the Grateful Dead when he should have been at Penn State, or in a bad spot out West with wild friends, he always knew we were in his corner. If he needed to, he called, and we got him back home.

Jeremy, our youngest, like his mother and brothers, was into music. I love that about the kids. They all sing. Jayson and Jeremy write and produce music as well as play keyboards, bass, drums, and guitar. Between the two of them they are a band. However, as a parent, I was very concerned about Jeremy, not because it was rock music that he was into, but because it was rock music on steroids. The lyrics, when you could make them out, were often dark and depressing, the artwork on album covers often scary. He always played it loud. As a student of music, I learned that music is sound placed in time. But this often sounded like noise and people yelling. But my inner child said, "Chill. Just because you can't hear the melody or dance the boogaloo to it, doesn't make it bad." Then I remembered being scolded for singing the lyrics to a song called, *Dang Me*. It put it all in perspective for me.

One of the many blessings in our life came when our youngest came to live with us full-time. His father had passed on and changing schools and leaving friends didn't seem as important to him. So Donna and I made the drive to mom's house to pick him up. This time he came not for the weekend, but to stay; and we quickly went from being fun moms to real parents.

I loved when Jeremy brought his friends home. I liked that we knew his friends, where they lived, and where the kids hung out. They were all skaters and very fond of skateboards. As parents, we had to set limits, which was the hard part. But the hardest part was enforcement. *Be in by 10:00 pm*, a reasonable curfew, we thought. Growing up, my curfew was dusk and lightening bugs. Well, the thing about limits is that kids like to push them, even break them. We had warned Jeremy that if he didn't come home when he was supposed to, we would come get him. He repeatedly ignored this limit.

One night it got to be very late. Donna and I had to get to bed because we had to get up early for work. Ten thirty, no Jeremy, eleven o' clock, still no Jeremy. Donna and I got in the car in search of Jeremy. It didn't take long. As expected, from the car we saw him hanging with his friends in front of his best friend's house. He stood, rocking his skateboard, with his friends in various positions, sitting on the stoop and talking. It looked like a scene from a coming-of-age movie.

"Jeremy," I called to him. At first he seemed not to hear me. "Oh, Jeremy," I called again.

I am sure he could tell by my tone that I had reached my limit. He got in the car. We were both angry, but we survived. Donna drove us quietly home. I think thirteen is a hard age.

Jeremy had a teacher, Mrs. Young, who seemed to be very hard on him, even unfair. It seemed no matter what he did or how hard he worked, he could not do well enough for this teacher. I needed to talk to her and see Mr. Aces, the principal about another pressing matter.

I went to the school to see the principal about the fact that Jeremy's locker had been broken into, some things were stolen, and someone wrote *nigger* on his locker door. The principal assured me that the situation would be investigated and handled. However, the teacher I wanted to see was not available. Two days later, I got a phone call from the school. This teacher was requesting a meeting with me. I told her that I wanted to speak with her also, and we set the appointment.

When I arrived at the school, I went directly to the classroom assigned to Mrs. Young. A woman of average height with dark hair greeted me. She had an air of snootiness about her. She was kind of cold and barely shook my hand.

I smiled and said, "I have some concerns about how Jeremy is doing in your class."

She responded by explaining, "Black males have to fight and work very hard to make it in this world, and Jeremy is not grasping this concept."

After I picked my jaw up off the floor, I said, "I believe it is hard to make it in this world no matter what your background is. Jeremy and I both feel that you are harder on him than the other kids."

She didn't miss a beat and said in a very accusatory manner, "Someone has to be. Your son is not in touch with his blackness and is unprepared to go out into the world as a black man. You allow him to listen to rock music, and he is not familiar with the music of his people. He knows very little about rap."

I wanted to speak, but I couldn't. Shock then anger, then just anger.

She went on. "You allow him to straighten his hair," she said, as she looked judgingly at my hair, which was nap free. Her hair was pulled back but looked pretty straight to me. "You allow him to ride skateboards, and you listen to classical music in your home."

"I have had enough," I said. "First of all, you are way out of line. My son is in the eighth grade. No eighth grade kid is prepared to go out into the world as a man, no matter what color they are. He listens to the music he likes, and if you want to get specific, the music of *his people* is gospel. Yes, we listen to classical music at home. We listen to all kinds of music at home. As his mother, I allow him to make choices, and he chooses to straighten his hair. He likes it. So do I. Jeremy and his friends of all backgrounds ride skateboards like most American kids his age. I suggest you turn your attention to teaching. What goes on in my home and how I raise my child is none of your business. Conversely, what goes on in this classroom is my business. Your approach to teaching is racist and grossly unfair and that is just the beginning of my complaint to the school board. I strongly suggest that you immediately find a way to cope with the person my son is, and your new approach better be reflected in his grades, which you may want to review in light of this meeting."

With that said, I headed straight to the principal's office and gave him a heads up. "I am on my way to the Board of Education building to complain about the racism in your school, not just the students, but also your faculty.

The undercurrent of racism perpetuated by the teachers is being consciously or unconsciously taught to the students."

The principal tried, but did not have a chance, to get a word in. I said my piece and left.

When I arrived at the school board offices, there was no one in authority to speak with. This just made me angrier. By the time I got home, I had two messages from the school principal and one from the office of the superintendent. I guess the superintendent got the message I left for him. I returned both calls the next day. We had a meeting to discuss the matters. I am happy to say that the school did take steps to work out their diversity problems. The staff and students participated in workshops and my son's grades improved. His teacher was disciplined and was forced to attend further trainings. Sometimes, you just have to draw the line. Mine is easy. Do not mess with my kids, my mom, my love, my family.

We hadn't told our families that we were a couple right away. Everyone considered us roommates. We lived in a five-bedroom home. No one questioned our living arrangement, at least not to my face. This worked for us because the transition from traditional relationship to a same sex relationship was not always a smooth ride, mostly because of outside issues and other people. It took a long time for us to get on the same page about who could know, and when we would be open about our relationship.

I was heavily involved with my church, which was an added problem for me, and Donna was just uncomfortable about the whole idea because of her family and society's treatment of gay people. It became clear to me that I really only cared about three things with regard to who knew about us: my God, my mom and my kids. I knew that God was cool with us because he sent Donna to me. Well, obviously God knew. He knows everything. It made sense to me that once my mom and my kids knew, the world at large didn't matter. Anyway, it was none of their business.

When Donna and I finally decided to tell our families, the reactions were not what we expected. My mom simply said, "I know." My kids had varying reactions ranging from silence to, "Two girls? Cool. Does this mean that I can ask her for money to go to the movies?" Donna's mother didn't say much and hugged her. Her father, on the other hand, said, "If you are going to be with a woman, did you have to pick a black one?" Yes, her father won the award for most outrageous reaction. He was not at all bothered by his daughter's same sex relationship. He was bothered by the fact that the relationship was interracial.

My family welcomed Donna with open arms. She was part of the family from day one and even more so once we were open about our relationship. Donna's family's treatment of me was a stark contrast for the most part. Donna's mother, Sylvia, and her mother's mother, Springie, never said an unkind word to me. Donna and I would visit, and we just didn't talk about it.

Springie was one of the sweetest people you could ever meet. She was a bouncy, bubbly person, always smiling. She had silver grey hair that was always perfectly in place. Springie was thin and small framed, a perfect grandma size, and beautiful inside and out. She was always trying to convince me and Donna of the benefits of carrot salad, which she made often. It seemed that every time we had dinner at Springie's house, a side of carrot salad with raisins was included. Goodness oozed from this woman.

Donna's mom was a nurse, although she stopped working when the kids were small to take care of her family. One could see where Donna got her looks from. Her mother was athletic, played tennis, and enjoyed canoeing and photography. She had short blonde hair, bright blue eyes. As a child, Sylvia was a model in an ad campaign. Sylvia and Springie treated me nicely.

The father, Donald, was chief pathologist and coroner over the two local hospitals. Her father, Donna's brother, Jeff, and grandmother, Dorothy, were not so nice. Their physical appearances complimented their mean dispositions. The two men had dark hair and dark eyes. I rarely saw them smile.

Her fraternal grandmother, was the complete opposite of Springie. She was a large woman with grey hair mixed with dark. Her eyes were dark. I never saw her smile. She always tried to use her wealth to get Donna to break up with me. She once said, "You better know who butters your bread." Those kinds of comments were lost on Donna, but she used them anyway.

This side of the family referred to me as common and her brother just outright called me a nigger. These were not easy times for Donna or our relationship. There were constant phone calls and threats to disown her. They went so far as to find a job for her and demanded she move home. Still, she stayed with me.

Donna's parents had marital issues. Her father, a raging alcoholic, was abusive to her mother, and having an affair with his secretary. We were happy for her mother when he moved out, and she filed for divorce.

When Donna's mother became seriously ill with pneumonia, Donna and I visited her in the hospital. We often took care of her. Donna and her mother became even closer during this time. Her mother even visited us at our home in Pennsylvania after that. When we visited her, she would take us to the yacht club just to spite her husband. We sat on his boat, so that everyone could see that there was a black person on his boat. She knew he would hate that.

Except for Donna's mother and maternal grandmother, her family was never at a loss for ways to hurt Donna or mistreat both of us. Donna was excluded from family things such as weddings and holiday gatherings more than not. I was never welcomed.

Donna's mother, became very ill again and was hospitalized a second time with a serious infection. Donna and I immediately rushed to the hospital. Her family treated Donna horribly.

Her uncle and father questioned, "You brought *her* here?"

Her uncle grabbed Donna by the collar, angrily inferring that our relationship somehow caused this and told me to leave.

Donna yanked his grip away from her neck, "Keep your hands off me," she sneered back, and we went outside.

That was enough of a spectacle in the hall of a hospital, we thought. In the days that followed, Donna visited her mother without me. It was for the best as she was stressed enough. Donna's mother passed three days after Christmas.

Donna was grieving, hurting, and there wasn't a thing I could do to fix it or make it better. At the funeral, Donna's father told her to get anything that was hers out of his house. Some time after the funeral, Donna went to the house to get her things, but when she arrived, he had locked her out and changed all the locks. How much more could this woman take? He couldn't wait until after the funeral to change the locks? Really, there are no words to describe him fully. He was so evil even Satan wouldn't want him.

Donna never got her things, her father kept all the items that her mother intended to be left for her, including her diamond ring. The parents were in the middle of a divorce when her mother died. Since it was not yet final, he was still, albeit only on paper, the husband and next of kin.

Her father wasted no time. Immediately after Sylvia's death, he gave up his rental and moved back into the house. A few weeks later, his secretary moved in, and they were married. We like to refer to her as EP, Executive Prostitute.

I don't know how Donna endured all this. But then there was more. Three weeks after her mother died, Springie left us. Six weeks after that, her great Aunt, Edith, died also. For months, we had been visiting Edith in the nursing home. We would make her home cooked meals and bring them to her. She loved that and our visits.

There was no family contact for a very long time after the funerals, until out of the blue, we received a birth announcement from Donna's brother, Jeff, and his wife, Helen. Donna had not spoken to her brother for several years. She was so happy to hear from a family member and to find out that she was an aunt. I was not so happy. I didn't trust it. However, we called and went to visit her brother and his family. Donna was so excited and just glowed when she held her niece. All of a sudden, I had in-laws of a sort.

They invited us for dinner, even Christmas dinner. I knew that I was being tolerated. I remember the look of hate in Jeff's eyes the day he called me a nigger. He hadn't found Jesus, so that didn't change. Donna sort of had family now, so I was not going to ruin that for her. I sucked it up and went along.

Donna's niece was still very young when Helen, Donna's sister-in-law, became pregnant with a second child. This was a difficult pregnancy, so she needed help with chores at home and at their automotive repair shop. Donna and I had full-time jobs and our own home but when asked, we gladly helped. Weekly, we drove down to their home and gave Helen a break. We watched the baby. We cleaned the house and sometimes helped with dinner. We also went to the shop to clean the waiting room and bathroom. I have to tell you, there were times that that restroom was positively gross. We were literally the family maids for quite some time.

Eventually we got to the point that we just couldn't do it anymore, and we didn't want to. Helen had the baby. We helped out during the whole pregnancy and for a long time after that. My feeling was, if you could go back to work, which she did, you were fine. Besides, the whole time we helped out, they really could have afforded a cleaning service for the business and their home. Their income bracket was way above ours.

We were still occasionally invited for dinner and things were going along just fine. We even threw Jeff a birthday party at our home. Jeff and Helen came to our home with the two kids many times for dinner and cookouts. Maybe I did have in-laws after all. Donna had her nieces whom she loved spending time with.

Not too long after, Donna's father died. I can't say I was sad. Donna received a call from an attorney who gave her a copy of the will and informed her that she was acknowledged only in that she had been left nothing, which was sick but expected. Donna was hurt even though she knew this would be the case.

Now EP would have all her mother's things and all the family money. It appeared that she wasted no time. We were told that her ex-husband moved into the house before the funeral was even over. I always thought that EP had this planned the whole time. She knew that Donna's father had a drinking problem and a bad heart. He died of a heart attack. Case closed.

Her father's mother, Dot, as I like to refer to her, died also, leaving Donna out of her will as promised because Donna refused to break up with me and move home.

Donna and I had now been together many years. My grandmother told me years before that if a relationship lasts five years, it is good and solid. So for our fifth anniversary, I put Donna's name on the house. Later, when available in New Jersey, we got a domestic partnership. As soon as Civil Union became available, we got one. It was the closest thing to being married. Moving forward, Donna tried to legally adopt my three children, but Pennsylvania would not allow that unless I would give up my parental rights. We were trying to be a family. I certainly wasn't willing to give up my kids. Finally, several years later, while living in New Jersey, the law changed and Donna legally adopted the three boys. Because they were not young children and over eighteen, they had to give their consent, which they did. We were a real family, as much as the law would allow. Gay marriage was a long way off. Some people didn't think it would ever happen.

With everything going so well between Donna and her brother, it never occurred to us that he would be unhappy about our now legal family, but he was more than unhappy. He was furious. He called Donna yelling and screaming. I could hear him across the room. He was upset that Donna had adopted the kids.

He kept yelling, "It's not legal. I am taking you to court. I am seeing my lawyer in the morning."

Well, he was angry because by adopting my children, they became grandchildren. This meant that they had a standing in the will. Apparently, when EP leaves this world, one of the trusts that she has been receiving the interest from to live on, gets divvied up between the grandkids. He expected his two girls to get it all. Even though he kept referring to it as his money instead of his children's money.

Funny thing, Jeff pissed the father off one day by commenting that he didn't think EP took good care of his children when she watched them and requested that she did not have the baby lay on the floor with the dog. Her hurt feelings were all it took for this man to leave his son out of the will, also. Think about it, this multi-millionaire did not leave his two children one cent, and for no good reason. How does that play in his head? *My daughter lives with a nigger, and my son doesn't like the way my new wife babysits; so I will cut them out of the will.*

Jeff would not let go of this. He told Donna he would only consider speaking to her again if she had the boys sign away their right to any money that may or may not be left when EP dies. The way things were going, there wouldn't be anything left but the proceeds from the house when it was sold. Jeff had no reason to worry about his kids; he is a multi-millionaire in his own right. His kids will inherit that. Plus, the kids were to become Ivy League graduates. They would do well on their own. Again, I was relegated to the negative, a color, a bad word. That hate in his eyes went clear through. Only God could change his heart. So Donna once again lost her family. She was heartbroken at the loss of her nieces whom she loved and adored.

Three years later, while at the doctor's office, I could tell that Donna was not entirely with us as I sat with her and Doctor Pratt to discuss the probability of cancer. The very thought of it was life changing. Donna developed breast cancer. What an ugly word, cancer. I hate it more than nigger, more than any other word. I noticed that the doctor was directing everything to Donna instead of to both of us. She barely acknowledged my presence and seemed annoyed when I asked questions.

On the morning of my fiftieth birthday, the call came. I answered the phone. It was the doctor. She wanted to speak to Donna. I stated that I was Donna's partner and that she should tell me the findings, but she refused. She would only talk to Donna. I reminded her of the HIPPA forms that clearly give Donna's permission to discuss her health with me. Donna was on an emotional edge. I believed whatever the news, it would be better coming from me. Also, Donna had a tendency to zone out when this topic was discussed. I was sure she would miss some important information that she didn't want to hear. It didn't matter to the doctor what I thought, she refused to talk to me.

Donna sat next to me. She had no choice but to take the call. The doctor told her that she definitely had breast cancer, and that it was worse than she'd initially thought. When she hung up, I knew. She had a blank stare. I just hugged her. There were no words. After a while, we remembered that we were expecting a houseful for my fiftieth birthday party.

"We have to cancel the party," I said. "I am not really in the mood for a party, and I am sure you aren't."

"Oh, no," Donna insisted, "we are having a party." So we both took a deep breath, and pretended all was well.

We returned to the doctor. Dr. Pratt and I didn't like each other. I had come to think that her issue was with our relationship.

"I prefer you are not in the room during our consultation," she said coldly.

"I want her with me." Donna held her ground.

The doctor was forced to talk to both of us, not just Donna. The cancer was already in her lymph nodes and they feared it may have traveled other places. Arrangements were made for the surgery, a mastectomy followed by chemo and radiation. The surgery went well. The treatment was harsh and aggressive.

Donna was often sick from the chemo. She couldn't eat most of the time. The smell of food often made her sick. I took care of her. Sometimes, I would sneak outside and sit in my car and cry and holler. It hurt so much to see her like this and suffering. I felt so helpless. I'd pray.

One day I came downstairs and found Donna on the couch. I spoke to her. She didn't answer. She looked so lifeless lying there. I was so scared. I tried to wake her. Her breathing was so shallow. She opened her eyes. *Thank you, Jesus*. It seemed like the chemotherapy was killing her. Finally, it was done, now radiation. After four months of chemo and six weeks of radiation, we meditated and prayed it would all work. It did. At this writing, she is ten years' cancer free, thank you, God!

During this time, I contacted Donna's brother Jeff to let him know how sick she was. We had almost lost her. I called his house many times and left messages. I called the shop, I sent emails and letters. No response. I contacted his in-laws who lived next door to him. Helen was his mother-in-law's name also. Helen senior answered when I called. It had been weeks since I had started leaving messages and sending letters. Helen was shocked to hear about Donna's illness. I knew they ate meals together every day. So evidently, he had never said a word. Helen insisted that her daughter and son-in-law didn't know. We both knew that wasn't true. She agreed to go next door and tell them immediately. Till this day we have not heard a word from Donna's nieces, brother, or sister-in-law. Helen senior never spoke to us again either. *Sick, twisted and sad.*

Still, *we made it through the rain,* as Barry Manilow sings.

Donna and I rarely lived alone in our five-bedroom home. We were always trying to help people out. Everyone is welcome. We surely had the room. Even Georgette, the barmaid at the Stonewall, lived with us for a while. There was never a dull moment. Donna always said that life with me was not boring. When we became us, I came with family and a large diverse group of people with varying degrees of importance in my life. I was very involved in my church as a cantor, choir member and bible school teacher. This gave me a whole set of people in my life that were totally different from drag queens and all things that, at the time, were stereotypically gay. Yes, we are the straightest gay couple I know.

If Wishes Were Horses,
Beggars Could Ride

I AM OLD SCHOOL. I TRULY LOVE MY FRIENDS. OFTEN THEY ARE like family to me. Sometimes people do not understand that. People often wonder why or how I could be friends with certain people. However, people who know me do understand. I try not to judge. My friends do not have to always agree with me, like what I like, or believe what I believe. I love them anyway. It is their heart that captures me, the good in a person. When I look into a friend's eyes and see clear to their soul, I see beauty and goodness. I see love. That doesn't mean that we will never have cross words or be angry at each other. It is assurance that the discord will pass, and our friendship will go on forever. Love is forever, and I truly love my friends.

Many times in life you find that, in retrospect, a seemingly meaningless and ordinary moment was really extraordinary. Several years before I met Donna, such a moment happened when the guys came over for our usual Saturday fun and frolicking. We were having a great time when the doorbell rang.

I heard a voice from the kitchen yell, "Oh that must be Marc. We invited him. Didn't think you would care."

I was wearing a sparkling lavender choker sweater that tastefully showed a little cleavage, when I opened the door to a very youthful looking, boyish man who had thick blonde hair, clear blue eyes and a sweet smile.

"Hi, I 'm Marc."

"Hi, Marc, I'm Leticia. Come on in."

Before I could step aside, Marc darted forward, buried his head in my cleavage, and kissed my chest. "You have lovely little necks," he said.

I laughed, "Well you fit right in with this group!"

Although, he did fit in the group, because he was young, good looking, and gay, he was very different from the other guys. We made an instant connection. Marc was funny, though his jokes were often thought provoking or dark. He was warm. His inner child was always out, often hiding his intellectual prowess. He was clearly a thinker with a quick wit. The laughter continued until the usual departure time, but Marc didn't leave with the others. We hung out and talked.

The next day, the phone rang. It was Marc. He called to thank me for a fun evening and asked if I wanted to go to the movies.

"Well, sir, I am a married woman with children," I replied in a *Gone with the Wind* kind of voice.

"Frankly my dear, I don't give a damn," he replied. We laughed.

"I would love to, but I have to see if my mom will watch the kids."

My husband was out with his friends. I worked a forty-hour week, carried a full load at school, and still had to be a wife and mother.

We went to the movies then came back to my house for a bite to eat. We talked for hours. It turns out that we both grew up within the same religion, as Mennonites, one of the many different protestant religions that emphasize adult baptism among other things. Marc was a philosophy major but had taken time off from school. We became fast and best friends.

One day he said to me, "If you were a man, you would be perfect for me."

"Well, I wish you were a different kind of man because you are perfect for me; but I am married and you are gay." When my marriage was over we did try but we made better friends and great housemates.

Marc was the only Super Jock that I remained close friends with as the years passed. Sometimes he acted like a protective father, especially regarding my dates. Donna was the only person he ever liked that I dated. He was insanely and over-the-top opposed to my relationship with Ken, with good reason.

Marc got me through some very difficult times. When things were not so good at home, he would listen to me, dry my tears and offer refuge. He loved steak sandwiches and having his back scratched. We were there for each other. Marc was right there holding me up when I needed it, and I was always there for him. I listened and often held him as he cried because of some guy who treated him badly. We spent a lot of time discussing his relationship with a Lutheran minister who constantly cheated on him. Sometimes we would just cry together. We shared our deepest and wildest thoughts and dreams.

Marc empathized while I ranted and cried about the pair of woman's underwear that I found in my apartment, under my bed, that weren't mine. One day, Marc helped me keep it together when I came home from work to find my husband holding our baby while smoking pot with his friends. After I grabbed the bag of pot and flushed it down the toilet, I wrapped up the baby and went to mom's house. But I could never tell my mother bad things that went on in my marriage as she was against the marriage from the start. So, over to Marc's apartment I went.

As always, we talked for hours. I opened up about what it felt like when I was in labor with my youngest and my husband came to visit. It was a difficult pregnancy. I went into labor, but the baby wasn't moving into place so there was a possibility of a C- section with complications. I was in a lot of pain and very scared. They had me hooked up to all kinds of monitors and gadgets.

My husband came in the room. He took one look and thought I was dying. I was just comforted that he was there. His tears were normal. We were having a baby, tears of joy. Well, not exactly. Thinking he may not have another chance, he decided to clear his conscious by telling me he had sex with another woman. *Really!* This takes bad timing to a new level. Actually, I was in way too much pain to care at the time. The nurses came to move me to the OR. They had to take the baby. While moving me to the operating table, the baby was born naturally in mid-air! It was still one of the best days of my life. Marc listened intently and helped me come to the obvious conclusion that my husband and I were too young and not ready for commitment or marriage. I thought, not at all like the soaps.

Sometimes, Marc would share deep and dark thoughts that often scared me, but I listened. He needed to talk about his thoughts and feelings. He often said there wasn't another person in the world he would tell the things he told me because they would have him locked up. He was right. I kept his darkest secrets. I still do.

When Marc was in his thirties, he joined the Navy. He loved ships and the sea. The opportunity to see the world and to belong to something so important was overwhelmingly appealing to him. He proudly and happily served his country. However, his country was not so wonderful to him. Being gay in the Navy was difficult at best. He literally lived two separate lives. It wasn't long before other military people noticed that he didn't have a girl-friend and wasn't looking for one. He didn't hang with the guys after hours.

On leave, he would come home to Donna and me and tell us how bad things were. We discussed what might help, like having a picture of a girl on the inside of his locker, any little thing that would say heterosexual. I was dec-imated by what I heard next. Marc wanted a picture of Donna instead of me because he thought the color of my skin would make things just as hard for him. Once he realized what he had said, he apologized. He knew I was hurt. I understood it all, but my inner voice heard, *he is ashamed of me.* I questioned the deep bond we had.

We came up with another idea. Maybe Marc should get married? Marc loved this plan.

"Then the guys wouldn't expect me to go out with women," he said. "I would have straight things to talk about. There would be visible proof that I am not gay."

He looked right at me and said, "Most people think we are a couple anyway, even our gay friends. We have lived together for such a long time. It's perfect."

What? I think he just asked me to marry him. My mind must be playing tricks on me.

After much discussion, Donna and I decided that I would marry Marc. It actually seemed pretty normal. Marc and I did love each other and had a very special bond that had already lasted years. Donna understood my connection to Marc and the level of our friendship. She had become a part of the friendship. Donna and I were not able to marry or even have a domestic partnership at the time. The piece of paper would not change anything or hurt us, and it would help him. So, I—we—married my friend. Marc would come home to our house when he was on leave and most weekends.

Several years passed. Domestic partnership became available to gay couples. Donna and I decided to get one, as it was the closest thing to a marriage at the time. I would now have to divorce Marc, so that Donna and I could take this legal step. After all, Marc and I were married long enough to dispel any gay gossip, and divorce was another straight topic that he could talk about as a cover. I called Marc, excited about the news that Donna and I were going take this big step.

I can still hear him saying, "I don't want a divorce." He wasn't joking. He asked why anything had to change. He liked being married. I was at a loss for words. It was not at all the conversation I thought we would have.

I started to remember how sometimes he snapped at me for no reason. He also had his demanding moments. Then there was one phone call in particular.

Ring. Ring.

"Oh, hi Marc."

"Where have you been? I have been calling you all day."

What? I could hear the anger in his voice. "Are you my husband or something?" I joked. "Because you are sounding very much like a husband," I laughed.

"Well, we are married, my lovely." Silence, then a giggle. We were okay.

But we weren't okay. Donna and I just didn't realize it. Marc was hurt that I wanted a divorce and didn't understand why things just couldn't stay the same. I explained that the law had changed, so Donna and I wanted to do this.

He asked, "What about me?"

"Marc," I explained, "nothing is changing but paperwork. We still love you. Nothing's really changed."

The divorce was easy from a legal standpoint. Emotional, not so much. Marc stopped coming home to Donna and me when he was on leave and on weekends. He made excuses as to why we couldn't visit him. Usually the excuse was that his parents were going to visit, or he had to work. His phone calls were further and further apart. I tried. I think he tried, but, in retrospect, I think he felt abandoned. I think he loved me in a way he didn't understand. I think he had fallen in love with me the day he said I would be perfect for him if I were a man.

We actually lost track of Marc. He changed his number and then moved. He always knew how to reach us but never did. He retired from the Navy.

One day, I got a call from church saying that someone was trying to reach me. The last name was the same as Marc's, but I didn't recognize the number. *Oh, Marc finally!* I called the number. It wasn't Marc. Marc's family had an issue with the color of my skin, so there was little to no contact, even when we lived together.

"I am Marc's sister in-law," a voice said. *I had never met his sister in-law.* "We have been looking for you Leticia," she said. "We found your picture and CD under Marc's bed."

"Who are you?" I asked.

"We buried Marc two weeks ago. He had been sick for some time."

"What! Why didn't someone call me?"

"We couldn't find you."

"My number hasn't changed. You found me now."

"You have to understand," she went on, "we didn't know Marc ever married. His mother took the news that he married you very hard."

"So you waited till he was dead and buried to call me! Where is he? Where did you bury him? And why are you calling me now?"

"Listen, we are trying to take care of things. Marc left you something. Call this man at this company."

I felt like somebody punched me very hard in the chest. I got cold. My body felt kind of numb. Tears came. So much left unsaid. We never talked, never said goodbye. He just disappeared from our lives and now he was gone.

Marc's sister in-law called a few more times because she had questions, or maybe she hoped I would turn whatever it was that he left me over to the family. She told me that Marc wouldn't go to the doctor or a hospital, that they had tried for months to get him to go. Months? She stopped calling after I said, "He should have come home to me and maybe he would still be alive."

Donna and I went to Indiantown Gap National Cemetery where they buried Marc. It was so sad. We drove through the gates past the large stone wall bearing a military seal. I tried not to cry. It started to rain. He was put in the new area, which was a little muddy at this point. Donna covered us with an umbrella as we walked to his spot. I felt a smile cross my face. I felt oddly at ease.

I heard him say, "I thought you would never get here."

And I replied, "Well, if it takes forever . . ."

I looked around. Just me and Donna, but I felt him there with us. Donna decided to wait in the car for me. She knew Marc and I were going to chat. And we did. It was just like the old days when we first met. He didn't answer all my questions, but he gave me peace and closure with jokes and song.

His favorite song was *Shiver Me Timbers*. I sang a bit to him and said goodbye to my friend.

Yes, it is a person's heart that captures me, the good in a person. When I look into a friend's eyes and see clear to their soul, I see beauty and goodness. I see love. That doesn't mean that we will never have cross words or be angry at each other. It is assurance that it will pass, and our friendship will go on forever. Love is forever and I truly love my friends.

I Had Some Friends but They're Gone

OUR FRIEND, JESS, HAD A TIMESHARE IN THE MOUNTAINS AT A SKI resort not far from us, an hour drive. He invited us to come up for a few days in January of eighty-seven to get away, so we did. We had no idea what an adventure this would lead to.

The resort was typical in that it had lovely grounds, a main area with games, entertainment, a pool, and a social department that hosted planned activities. On our second day there, they hosted a trip to the local bowling alley. Participants were told to drive to the meeting place, and then we would caravan to the designated destination. Donna and I, along with Jess and others, piled into the car and took our place in line. It was winter and a bit cold, but still a beautiful sunny day. We got out of the car as many did, and we waited for the trip to start. There were a few kids, but mostly adults.

As we waited, another car lined up behind us. It was a big, beautiful, Buick Riviera, metallic gold in color. The car seemed a bit out of place, more high-end than any of the others. We were admiring the car when the door opened. Cowboy boots and a full-length fur stepped out. Underneath the coat was a very tall, attractive, suntanned, blonde haired man with fabulous sunglasses and a great smile. He was joined by another man in a very cool leather jacket and equally cool sunglasses and also a woman who was oddly dressed like the rest of us, not at all glamorous. We speculated about who they might be. They looked and acted like rock stars. Well, that was a possibility since we were close to New York City, and the car had New York plates. This was a resort, after all.

When we arrived at the bowling alley, the resort staff divided us into teams and assigned lanes. Our lane was on the opposite side of the room from the rock stars. I wasn't surprised since there always seemed to be drama around us, although not so much from us. Donna says life with me is never dull, and she is never bored. Sometimes, Donna comes along for the ride because she loves me.

Donna was a very quiet, low-key person, almost shy. That is why, when she would, on occasion, assert herself or vent, I was completely surprised and would ask, "Who are you and what have you done with Donna?"

Donna was a Clinical and Industrial Psychology major with a minor in photography. She enjoyed swimming and playing tennis, both of which she continued in college. I was her complete opposite: outgoing, assertive, and sometimes a force. I started out as a psychology/sociology major that changed to nursing, but ultimately, I graduated with a BA in music. Some would say we were the odd couple, but not in the same way as Felix and Oscar. I have often said that our relationship was not perfect, nothing is, but it was and is the closest thing to it. Twenty years ago, I couldn't imagine my life without Donna. Now add fifteen years, I still can't. I don't want to.

Well, we were supposed to bowl three games, but I twisted my wrist during the first game and was forced to sit out the rest. Luckily, there were video games to play. I headed straight for the trivia game. I love trivia games. While I was playing the game, I suddenly realized that someone was in my space. I looked up and found that I was being watched. Standing beside me was one of the guys we saw earlier in the caravan line. He was the driver of the Riviera with NY plates. I recognized the stunning leather jacket and sunglasses that were now perched on his head. I noticed immediately that he was very attractive. He had a full head of dark brown wavy hair. His eyes were full of childlike wonder. But he was clearly not a child.

He said, "I noticed you stopped bowling."

"I had to," I replied. "I hurt my wrist."

"I needed a break," he said. "Are you from the area?"

"No, vacationing with friends." I continued playing the trivia game. I like games, and I am pretty good. There was a slight pause, then I looked at him.

"I'll play you a game of trivia," he quickly said.

I can't believe a man is trying to pick me up at a bowling alley.

"My name is Felix."

"Leticia, and sure, let's play." I know how to flirt too, I thought. So we bantered and flirted as we played trivia. I must say it was fun, the trivia game and the game we were playing. As we became more comfortable with each other, the conversation got more real and personal. I kind of liked him, and he made it clear that he liked me. Then it got weird.

"What do you do?" he asked.

"I'm a singer," I said simply. I never answer that question with my day job. I answer with my career.

He stared at me strangely and said, "I'm a record promoter."

Well this must be the daddy of all pick-up lines, really! We continued to play trivia and talk.

"I would love to help you," he said, handing me his card. "Call me Monday. I am staying at Shawnee Resort over the weekend."

"I know."

"How did you know I was at Shawnee?" he asked.

"We are on the same bowling trip!" I said, putting the card in my pocket. We both laughed. Then things felt more relaxed for some reason. "You, your friends, and gorgeous car stood out in the caravan. Everyone noticed you."

He laughed. "Let's meet later for drinks."

Just then Donna came over. "This is Donna, my partner."

We were joined by the tall blonde in the big fur coat. Felix completed the round when he introduced his partner, Michael. We both looked at each other and had a conversation with our eyes. *You're gay? You're gay? Let's be gay together!* We exchanged villa information and left.

When we returned to our villa, I explained the meeting to Donna and our friends. I told them how he suddenly became a record producer after I told him that I was a singer. I wasn't born yesterday. He was a lot of fun, though. Our friend, Jess, suggested that we invite them over for drinks instead of meeting somewhere. Donna and I both thought this was a good idea. After all, they were strangers, although there were moments I felt like I had always known Felix. It was weird. We kind of clicked.

I had written his villa information on the back of his business card. I took it out and read the card. It had his name followed by the title, *VP Promotion,* a phone number, address, and the company logo of Sony records. We were all in shock.

"Well," I said, "anyone can make a business card. It proves nothing. Anyway, what are the chances, really, that a singer just happens to meet a record company executive in a bowling alley? Now add to that the chances that I would meet a record executive at a bowling alley in the mountains of Pennsylvania."

"Call the phone number," someone said. So I did.

Dialing. Ringing.

"Good afternoon, Sony records," said the voice on the other end of the phone. I sat down and stumbled for words.

"Felix Meir, please."

"Mr. Meir is out of the office until Monday. Can I take a message?"

"No, no message, thank you." Well, we all had a good laugh at my expense and decided that we better serve good wine and great hors d'oeuvres when they came.

While it was somewhat exciting to think that we were going to be par-
tying with a record company executive, once Felix and his entourage, Michael
and their friend Lori, arrived, it didn't matter at all. We had a fun time with
fun people, and the party moved to the local gay nightclub where we danced
till the club closed down for the night.

It was the beginning of an intense, fun filled, fast paced, and, at times,
beautiful, seven-year friendship, almost like a marriage. The four of us spent
a lot of time together, playing cards on free weekends, going to concerts, dinners, vacations, holidays, even visiting with family.

Donna and I were suddenly living two very different lives. There was
the 8:00 a.m. to 4:00 p.m. job, working with people with developmental
disabilities; in contrast to, gigs with my accompanist or band, parties at a
disco diva's house, Oscar parties with record executives, and hot clubs where
Grace Jones performed. I have to say that woman was wild. We were standing
in front of the stage. The place was packed. Grace was doing her thing very
well on the stage when suddenly she danced and sang her way to the person
standing next to me, did a full squat and pushed the man's face between her
legs. "Have a little Grace in your face," she said.

I about died. I was still recovering from her top. It was a pair of sus-
penders that covered each of her nipples. Yes, that was it. It was a wild night.
When we went to the after-party backstage, she was so different. She shook
my hand and said, "Nice to meet you."

Through Felix I met Carole King, whom I adore. She was going to be
at Jones Beach Theater. I had never been to Jones Beach in Long Island, and
it is not an easy drive from where we lived. But it was worth all the traffic and
crazy drivers it took to get there. We picked the guys up in Manhattan, and
we were on our way.

The venue is heavenly, truly heavenly with the ocean as part of the
experience. It is an open-air theater. As usual, Felix got us wonderful seats.
We were right by the water but also close to the stage. The temperature was
just right with the ocean breeze. The moon was full and high. The music was

awesome. Each note seemed to float on a breeze of its own. I sang along with every one of them. So did mostly everyone else. Being a big fan, I have performed many of Carole's songs.

After the concert, we followed Felix and Mike through a maze of doors, stairs and platforms to backstage. Finally, there were people. They were drinking and munching and talking. I didn't know anyone, but I was happy to be there. While we were talking, a very small-framed woman walked toward us, drying her hair with a towel. She apologized for keeping people waiting. It was Carole. Felix made the introductions. Donna and I were so thrilled to meet her. She is such a prolific songwriter.

On my return to this venue with Felix and Mike, we saw Bonnie Raitt, who we have seen several times. We enjoy her, and she was touring to support her *Nick of Time* album. Every Bonnie Raitt concert is a gem. On this night at the after party, I again congratulated her on a wonderful concert. She responded, "Leticia, nice to see you again. Tish, you really should get a life." Yes, I had been to so many of her concerts that she knew my name, too funny. It was the oddest thing to be out till 2:00 a.m. at after parties, then get up and go to work after you were just eating pizza with Bonnie.

One afternoon, I got a call at work, and they called me in the office to take the call. The office staff listened in amazement while I confirmed plans with Felix to meet him and Donny Osmond for dinner at a Japanese restaurant in the city. It really was like having two lives. Donna and I said that all the time.

I am sure you are asking what happened to the beautiful friendship that was almost a marriage. Well, you know that whole thing about people coming into your life for a reason and a season? The seasons changed, and we got a painful but friendly divorce.

I continued to write and record music while working at the Developmental Center. I finished my CD in time for consideration in the

2000 Grammy Awards, which Donna and I attended in LA. It was another surreal experience, especially the red carpet. At the time it was most exciting to see my name in the same category, in print, listed under Cher's name. Again, it was like living two different lives.

Special Moments-
Awesome Wonders

AFTER DONNA'S BOUT WITH BREAST CANCER, WE BECAME VIGI-
lant about this disease; not that we were not before, just more so. There were
quarterly checkups for Donna and yearly checkups for me. True to form, we
scheduled our appointments so that we could go together.

On a very hot and humid day in August, we went to see Dr. Camal for
a follow-up visit after our mammograms. This time I was the patient. It was
just a small lump but needed to be checked. We both breathed a huge sigh of
relief when the doctor said she wasn't concerned at that time, but we should
watch it. It was my choice to have it removed now if I wanted. She gave me
a choice. Should I let them take a knife to my body or not? Well, we are still
watching it years later. I never really understood people who opt for surgery
if it is not a real issue. This includes elective surgeries. Surgery is serious stuff,
and people die in the simplest procedures.

With this good news, I sat up to get off the exam table and let out
a muffled scream. The doctor quickly turned around and asked, "What is
wrong?" as she headed back to the examination table. Donna grabbed my
hand and hugged me. We knew. I had been dealing with stomach pain off
and on. Most often, when I put my hand over the painful area and kneaded
it like bread, I could work it out. This time it caught me by surprise and was
infinitely more painful.

"I can see the issue from across the room," said Dr. Camal and put her hand squarely on it. "You have to see someone immediately. This is very serious."

Apparently, that kneading that I had been doing on my stomach was pushing my intestines back where they belonged. The doctor picked up the phone and made a call to another physician who deals with this sort of thing. As I listened to her speak to the other doctor, the reality set in. When I heard her make an appointment for me for the next day, I knew this was not good.

I reluctantly kept the appointment. The pain was gone. It always went away. Why bother, I thought. We are glad I bothered. In a matter of days, I was being prepped for surgery. This time, I wasn't given much of a choice. He told me if I did not have the surgery, I would die. This was life threatening.

Nothing is ever simple or easy with me. My surgery required two surgeons. It was really two surgeries. I must repeat, nothing is ever simple.

Late in the afternoon the day before my surgery, I received a call from one of the surgeons. "Your surgery is going to be canceled because your insurance company is not authorizing the procedure. They want to see pictures of the area I was going to operate on, but I cannot send them because the girl who does that, is not in the office. I tried to reason with them, but nothing could be done."

"What! I am going to die because you can't get pictures that you have in your office to the insurance company?" I thought my head would explode. "You said I would die if I didn't have surgery, and now you are going to let me die because you can't work it out with my insurance?"

"Calm down," he said. "You can pay for the surgery yourself. It will only be 9000 dollars, a mere fraction of the 27,000 dollars it would cost the insurance company."

What an education. There are two price lists, one for the patient if they are paying and one for the insurance company. "I don't have nine grand lying around," I replied, "I will have to make payments."

"Well, as self-pay, the surgery has to be paid in full up front," he replied.

"Really!" I suggested that I come and send the pictures to the insurance company, as I knew how. I could not believe that no one else in that office could scan and email photos. *You can't make this stuff up.* Of course, it was against policy for me to work behind the counter and send my own photos. Time was of the essence. I hung up and called Blue Cross Blue Shield who were no help at all.

I called the doctor back and tried to reason with him. After all, this was my life or death. He suggested that later that night I would be in a lot of pain. I should go to the emergency room for help. I would be admitted, and the surgery would then be covered by my insurance. *What?* I hung up in tears. This did not sound like a good plan to me.

Thankfully, the Lord is always working. An hour later, I got a call from the doctor's office. They were able to contact the person in the office who had the necessary skill to provide the pictures to the insurance company. She stopped by the office just before the close of business. The surgery was back on. *Crazy!*

The doctor assured me that they did this surgery all the time, and the up side was that I would get a bit of a tummy tuck. I found little comfort in that. Then he handed me several papers to sign, permission to treat me, bill my insurance, and, of course, a notice that anything could happen, even death. The second surgeon, Dr. Wilde would be handling the panniculectomy, while Dr. Boa would repair the hernia. The pannus, an apron of fat, had to be removed to get to the hernia. I don't know how long the surgery took.

When I woke up in recovery, it was comforting to see Jeremy and Donna at my bedside. I was very weak. I was cold, somewhat disoriented, and uncomfortable.

The next day, the doctor told me that while they were operating, it became necessary to rebuild my abdominal wall. A simple hernia repair turned into this huge surgery. The staff were concerned about my vital signs, which were taking a while to come back, so I was in recovery a long time. I was having trouble breathing, Donna and I both kept telling the nurses and the doctors.

They kept saying, "It's nothing serious," and gave me things to puff on and more pills.

As time went on, my breathing got worse. Well, they almost waited too long. All of a sudden, I found myself being rushed down the hall, nurses all around, hanging onto the bed, one holding an IV. I was scared. It was harder and harder to breath. I was so cold, so very cold. I could not speak. I was tired and weak. I heard, "Get her to CCU."

I thought, *God, am I dying? I am dying.* Just then I heard one of the nurses say, "We're losing her, we're losing her." I thought to myself, *I can hear you, asshole!*

My thoughts drifted to my family. I was so tired, but I was fighting to stay awake and alert. I was so cold. I just couldn't. The trip to the critical care unit seemed to take forever.

On the way, though, I felt two arms wrap around me. It was as if two arms came out of the blue, reached down, and hugged me. It was very comforting and best of all warm. I felt my body warm up. I wasn't cold anymore or scared. I no longer saw the nurses. I saw sky blue all around with spots of white. It was very bright, but there was no light as I have heard others speak of. I went to sleep.

When I woke up in CCU, Donna and Mom were at my bedside. I knew right away that God held me, as death passed me by. I didn't talk about it at first. I needed to process the whole experience.

I had a pulmonary embolism while they were treating me for anything but. Finally, they put in a filter and started me on Coumadin. So now my simple hernia operation had added excitement. *But wait.* Let's not forget that from the hospital I acquired a hospital infection so bad, that it took more than a week to realize it was really three different infections and required a drug cocktail to cure. I was very sick for a while, but I was alive.

When I was able to go home, I had the quiet and peace to contemplate all that had happened to me, God's gift, that hug and warmth—life. I knew that I had to share what happened to me. I didn't know what to do, so I asked to meet with my pastor. I was hoping he could explain what it all meant and what I could do. Well, it was clear that God had work for me to do. I would find a way to share this experience, this gift.

Church is so Full Of Sinners Christ Can't Get In

IN THE SUMMER OF 1993, DONNA AND I BOUGHT A HOME CLOSER to the shore area. I immediately went in search of a creative community. I answered an ad in the newspaper that was looking for singers to sing in a college alumni choir. This was odd to me since you didn't have to be member of the alumni, but I just wanted to sing and be involved with something. I called and made an appointment for an audition. I was given directions and noticed it was not far from the house.

When I arrived at Georgian Court University, I couldn't believe that such a beautiful place was hidden in the middle of this town, which was a mix of businesses and residential areas intertwined. When I made the turn off the main route, I noticed a large lake on my right. The homes were completely different from the street I turned off from, more upscale. Inside the college grounds were large impressive buildings, serene landscapes and very narrow roads with little parking.

The audition was also a bit of an interview. I earned a spot as a soprano and started that week. I enjoyed singing classical and sacred music. I had not sung in a choir of this type since high school. I made fast friends and before long was made an officer. Kelly, an alto in the choir, and I became good friends. She invited me to come with her to her church, Point Pleasant Presbyterian, to sing for the upcoming holidays.

I joined in her effort to help her church choir. They were singing the *Messiah*, which I love, and needed people to augment their choir. Of course,

I said yes. I had never been to a Presbyterian church before, but Presbyterians are Christians, so it worked for me.

From the first note, I was overjoyed. The director's style of conducting was much like my high school choir director's style. He was also friendly, flirty, and funny, to a point. It wasn't long before we became friends. It didn't seem to matter that I was the only black person in the choir. It was all about the music. That should have been a clue for me. A church choir should never be only all about the music. It also has to be about God, praise, and people. A church choir is another family you belong to. A church choir is about so much more than singing. But that is a topic for another time.

I came to notice that my new friend, Bill, was referencing my race or color constantly. Sometimes, I would tell myself it was a compliment or not personal. Sometimes, I would smile and laugh at the joke, even when it didn't quite sit right with me. After all, he was so nice to me, flirty, and friendly. I was flirty and friendly back. He always told me stories about one of his best friends, who is black. He told me over and over again, often in front of the choir, how Dorian was his "black brother." He was never just Dorian. I was enjoying singing the *Messiah* so much, and I was so caught up in all the attention that he gave me, that I let way too much slide.

By Christmas, I was a church regular, as I was also singing at the Sunday services leading up to the performance of the *Messiah*. I enjoyed choir folk and the music. So, when I was asked to stay and join the church, I did. The deciding factor for me was that the church participated in preparing and serving meals to AIDS patients. So many churches talk a good game but really do little or no service unless it benefits them in some way or they help church members only. I felt this was important work and special.

My friend, Bill, continued with what I now see as belittling racist mutterings designed to make himself feel good. He often gave me solos, always the Negro spirituals. He actually gave me an arrangement of a gospel medley and told me to help him, "black it up." Yes, I knew what he meant. However, at the time I was so thrilled that this very accomplished musician needed my help, I completely ignored the insult. After all, I was used to it.

One evening at choir, during what seemed to be a regular banter session, he actually referred to me as a lawn jockey during a rehearsal. Yes, *lawn jockey!* Suddenly, the sanctuary was silent except for the quiet outrage of a few of the choir members who spoke to me after rehearsal. I couldn't speak at first. I was so confused. *Is this man my friend or not? Is he a Christian?* The many remarks and comments and jokes at my expense stung. This hurt. I said to myself, *don't cry, just don't cry. Everyone is looking at you.* So I smiled as always and commented about his need to have me light the way. I thought to myself, *Lawn jockeys carry lanterns, and Bill was in the dark.* Bill quickly directed the organist to start playing.

A few weeks later, the choir director for the childrens and youth choirs quit. Bill approached me and asked if I would take the job. It wasn't a huge time commitment, and the pastor said they would work around any singing engagements that I had. Bill said he would be my boss. The kids would like me, they said. It turns out that the kids didn't like him. Apparently, he had directed those choirs in the past, and it did not go well. The kids stopped coming, and the choirs went by the wayside for the most part. I would be taking over what my predecessor was able to salvage.

I took the job. It was a way to give service by doing something I loved. I certainly was not doing it for the money. Also, Bill really was an outstanding director from whom I knew I could continue to learn. Bill and I maintained a friendship of a sort that worked and made working together easier.

I had made some changes in voice parts and chose music that younger Christians would like to sing, including a little folk, a little gospel, and some updated versions of traditional hymns. Parents began to ask me about signing up their children to sing in the choir. Both groups grew some. A large number of the members of the Youth Choir were seniors. However, they did not want to leave the Youth Choir to sing with Bill in the Chancel Choir. They were just going to drop out of music at church.

Katie and a few others asked, "Why can't we just stay in this choir?"

"Well," I said, "it would not be all youth in the choir because you will be finished with high school."

I thought about it and brought it up at a staff meeting. "I want to turn the Youth Choir into a Praise Choir and open it up to anyone who would like to sing," I proposed. "This way we would keep the kids that want to sing and are involved already. Some kids don't like classical or sacred music and do not want to sing it." There were also people who joined us that weren't involved in church activities and even a few from Bill's choir who chose to sing in both groups. However, Bill put a stop to that right away.

So, Voices of Praise was born. I gave the choir more gospel pieces to do. It was a joy! It was also not what people were used to, but the change was welcomed by most. They felt the spirit, and they saw the smiles on the faces of people lifting their voices together to praise God. Sometimes they gave me goosebumps. You could feel the collective spirit reaching to the congregation, sending messages of love, peace, and salvation.

Once the choirs really got going, I turned my attention to their choir robes. They were old and some very worn and stained. The children's robes were white and black, and the youth robes were a powdered blue. Both robes were very traditional and boring in style. I talked to Bill about getting new robes and showed him what I had picked for the new look. The choir had a new sound and a new purpose. It was a mission choir. Bill was very encouraging and seemed tickled pink that I was getting so involved. He said he liked the new robes, but that there was no money for them in the budget. If I could get the money, he had no problem with the purchase.

So I set out to get the money. I talked to the pastor, who made some suggestions. In no time at all, I had the money to get the robes. I had everyone measured and that was it, or so I thought. The robes were beautiful, purple, of course. The children's robes were a matching shade of purple to the Praise Choir robes with a white flowing tie that had a dove on it. The Praise Choir robes were purple and black, trimmed in silver with a silver cross on the left purple shoulder. There was also a matching overlay, with a large silver cross in the middle. They were fabulous.

A few weeks later, I was summoned into a meeting with church leaders. I was being reprimanded for buying the choir robes. *What?* I explained that I did not do this on my own without talking to people and getting permission. I explained why it was important to have them, and why our choirs needed them. Then without using the exact word, they called me a liar. Apparently, my supervisor, my friend, Bill, complained that I had gone rogue. He said he knew nothing about the choir robes prior to the purchase and that I had acted completely on my own, never involving or informing him of anything I did. The pastor, sitting in the room, was completely and oddly silent. I was humiliated and outraged. I decided to quit, but some choir members and the group's benefactor talked me out of it.

After this experience, Bill made regular complaints about me and my choirs. We didn't line the chairs up straight after rehearsals, our robes took up too much room, I was difficult to work with. I was told the Sunday school director had the same complaint.

Our choirs met on different nights and generally sang at different services. However, to my face, he and the Sunday school director were the same old friendly people, publicly singing my praises and Bill continued giving me solos. I tried to talk to Pastor about Bill and how he treated me, especially regarding the racial stuff and how he would undermine the Praise Choir. I was basically told to suck it up.

"Bill is a very well respected choir director and has been here many years. He brings in money. I am sure you are over reacting to the jokes."

Why did I bother? I told myself that I was doing God's work and kept on going.

Shortly thereafter, a coworker at my day job gave me a flyer about a gospel music festival. I was intrigued. One of the most talked about concerns at staff meetings was the lack of attendance, involvement and enthusiasm at our church. I saw this as a way to help with all of that and also get more people in the pews. Our mission, to lift the spirits of others and spread God's message through music, needed exposure and tools. *Voices of Praise* made a CD and entered a gospel competition.

It never occurred to me that an activity based in Christianity and fused with spirit filled music would be anything but welcoming and affirming. I completely missed the emcee's references to the black community. I thought they were talking about a Christian community. The comments that referenced "folks," weaves, and other ethnic references were noted but not taken to heart.

I remember arriving at the Theater with the Praise Choir. We were all so excited. We walked past another group of singers who were also waiting to check in. We were all finalists at this point, the cream of the crop. This was a huge deal for our choir and our church. As we walked by, the participants standing in line began to laugh and snicker. A choir member from the other camp reared back, put her hands on her hips, eyed us up and down, and commented, "What you gonna sing?" then continued laughing. *Wow, not very Christian like, I thought.*

I was already dealing with some fears within the choir. After all, we were a gospel choir from Point Pleasant, New Jersey with a ninety-nine percent white membership, singing in Newark, New Jersey, a much more racially diverse area with a large African American population. Some of the choir had never been to Newark, and their only reference was the six o'clock news. I believed we would be safe and treated well in a God centered activity, but the reality was, not really.

There were other instances where we were made to feel uncomfortable and even unwelcome. When we sang at the Theater at Madison Square Garden, while waiting backstage to perform, I overheard a conversation that was clearly meant for me to hear. "This is our competition," a woman said. "White people always trying to take from us. Now they are tryin' to claim our music. I can't believe that black woman brought them up in here."

My first inclination was to turn and address them face-to-face. However, we were back stage waiting to go on. I had to focus in order to keep the group focused. "Put it in the music," I said, and that's what we did.

When it was over, we had earned the respect of the other participants. When we did not take top prize, the group that won came to us and said, "You were robbed."

Yes, the white folks from Point Pleasant sang and performed their collective butts off. The other singers in the audience were up on their feet praising God and singing along. Some were standing on their chairs. Clearly, the audience did not expect to hear or see what they heard and saw. We were a wall of sound, tight and pitch perfect. The choreography was cool, and everyone was on top of their game. I was so proud of us because we worked very hard to get there.

It didn't take long for the excitement to leave and the racial reality to set in. There were hurt feelings all around and a sense of unfairness. It was clear that we were not wanted there; everyone got that message. The people working and running the competition did not do much of anything to make us feel welcome. That year and during the years that followed, there was always an issue with the microphones, or where we were supposed to stand, or with the lighting when we were performing. The group did not want to enter the competition ever again. They had had enough the first time. I explained to them that if we don't go back, bigotry would win. We had an opportunity to break down some barriers, to teach and lead. This is why we entered again and again.

We entered four or five more times, and each time we placed as a finalist but never won. The good news was that the way we were treated by some people improved. Most people did not look at us like we didn't belong anymore. I began to call us the Susan Lucci of this competition. It took her years to win her Emmy. Well, we had some fun, received medals and plaques, tried to move the racial issue forward in a positive way, and we let it be known that God's music is everybody's music. For our church, there was a new little buzz of excitement and pride. As one person said, we put the church on the map. There was national publicity, radio, and local press. The Praise Choir did bring some people to Point Pleasant Presbyterian Church.

We eventually made the decision to move on. It was clear that we would never take top prize, and the organization was making it harder and harder for us. I received a phone call from the production manager two weeks before what would be our last competition and show, telling me that we could not do the song we had worked on for nine months. It was crazy! We had paid for arrangements and music, and learned new choreography. It was two weeks till show time.

I was told, "It is her song, and she doesn't want your group singing it. She will sing it."

I remember thinking, *when did this gospel music competition become a vehicle for famous gospel acts instead of a competition for amateur groups that purports to uplift communities?* Anyway, she has sung this at this competition the last two previous years. This is not new material.

I was determined not to let them do this to us. It was the last straw. I got on the phone and explained to Darrel, who produced the track we would sing to, and who was also familiar with the gospel music industry and the people we were dealing with, what had happened. He explained how cut-throat the gospel music industry is and was happy to help.

We were just a little choir from Point Pleasant; who cared about us? In no time we had new music and a song to sing. We did not win. We still nailed it. Of course we did! That was one of the beautiful things about this group. They gave it their all and more. They felt each note on so many levels. They understood that music is a gift from God, and every heartfelt note that they sang had a purpose. Life is hard. They sang knowing that they were doing God's work by lifting the spirits of others and sharing his message of love and salvation. They knew that by blessing others, they also were blessed. On a competition stage or in a nursing home, this group understood their mission to provide food for the soul, and God gave us what we needed to do the job. Thank you, God!

A few weeks later, on Memorial Day weekend, I was out in my backyard preparing for a picnic when Donna yelled to me. I had a call that the answering machine picked up.

"You better come hear this," she said.

I ran into the house just in time to hear a well-known gospel-recording artist ranting about me doing her song, the same song she would not let us sing at the competition. "And who do you think you are?" the voice said.

Well, I guess I came to know who cared about our little Praise Choir. The person was clearly not in control of herself. I grabbed the phone, intercepting the answering machine, "Hello, I am Leticia can I help you?"

A loud voice on the other end of the phone said, "I know who you are. You're that black woman that brings that white group to gospel competitions. We all know who you are. I don't want you singing my song. Don't you know I can sue you?"

I had sent this person a CD of us singing the song in question because she was refusing to let us sing it at the competition. I believed that once she heard it, she would see that there was no solo performance in our version and no competition for her. I even suggested that we back her up at the next competition, and what an honor it would be.

I tried to explain to her that we had actually helped her increase her audience since we had introduced her music to a whole new group of people. Again, I pointed out the major differences in our version of the song, starting with the fact that ours was a group effort with no solo, no competition for her. She just kept ranting. I thought this was the most unchristian behavior ever, but then . . .

I was directing two choirs and singing in one. It was a real joy at first. As long as I knew my place, stayed in my place, and didn't complain about anything. I was a member of the church on paper but was never really treated as a person or member with equal standing. It occurred to me that I had never been asked to usher, be a deacon or serve on any committees. When I spoke on this, the pastor, and the assistant pastor, said they didn't think I would be interested.

So I began to show interest. Nothing changed. I continued to find my joy, my peace, and my spiritual food in the message of the music and serving God. Even when Bill threw a bulletin at me during a church service, I kept it together. After all, the pastor saw him do it and said nothing. I loved the choirs. The adults were like my siblings and my Doves were like my children. The congregation was my church family, for the most part.

In an effort to bring people, generations together, I suggested and started an arts program that I was soon forced out of. One of the problems with the way children and youth were handled was that they were regularly separated from not just the adults, but also the church. They were paraded out for big holidays and special occasions. I even had to fight to have the Dove Choir stay in church once a month when they sang. I was told that it was part of my job to teach these kids about the service, what to do, how to behave and so forth, however, they weren't allowed to be in the service. *Crazy, right?*

I had lots of suggestions and ideas but got stonewalled at every turn. Sometimes, the pastor would like an idea but then completely change the concept like he did with the arts program. In retrospect, I see what a narrow and self-serving vision the church was being led toward. The congregation had no idea, and the session was just the name of the group that was supposed to run the church. Really, they did the pastor's bidding, mostly without knowing it. He was that good—or bad—depending on your use of the words. Not all pastors are leaders. Preaching and leadership are different skill sets.

One Sunday between services, I was getting ready for the second service. Bill and his choir had just sung at the first service and were in the process of leaving. I had a small window of about a half an hour to rehearse the choir and for the choir to get their robes on. I often had to fight for every minute.

Bill always had to talk with me or interfere in some other way, clearly so we didn't get to go over our songs. However, he pitched a fit if I dared try and talk to him during his half hour of rehearsal time. So during the transition period just before that half hour start time, often there were members of both choirs in the choir room.

On this particular Sunday, Bill and I were bantering back and forth about music and church choirs, and I answered him back to a smart remark he made. He had no comeback.

So in front of everyone he said, "Yeah, well, I know what you do in bed."

The room went dead. My choir members gasped and looked at me. I had no words. His choir members put their heads down and left. I can't even articulate what it felt like. After all, I was at church. My sanctuary. You are supposed to be safe at church. I was just attacked. Bill left. The choir members who heard this tried to comfort me. That was the longest service.

When it was over, again I went to pastor and told him what happened. There were witnesses this time willing to come forward on my behalf.

He said, "What do you want me to do? Do you want me to talk to him? That could make things much worse."

I have no idea why I thought it would be any different. Why did I think he would care, or I would matter? I was so running out of cheeks to turn.

I asked for a meeting with both clergy. I thought, maybe they really didn't see the disparity in treatment or understand how things really were from my point of view. On the surface and publicly, they treated me fine. I set out to show them, complete with examples that our church engaged in institutional racism. I especially liked the very recent example of a staff meeting where everyone else was allowed to speak up and interject, but when I contributed I was publicly humiliated for speaking out of turn. I showed them example after example of how I was treated differently than the other staff. My choirs and activities were always the last consideration behind Bill's choirs, youth activities, and everything else.

I reminded them of the offer wherein the Praise Choir would take over care of the stage and big room in the education building, including painting, curtains and stage curtain, and cleaning, which was very much needed. Bill never wanted to share the choir room or an office with me, which is why I didn't have one. It made sense that the Dove and Praise Choir use this space in the education building. The stage, piano and sound system were all right there. I was told that the Boy Scouts met there and therefore my request was denied. *They met every day and Sunday?* I was accused of not being a team player. I think they should have let me on the team and watch the game before they accused me of that.

The Boy Scouts had a special place in the pastor's heart. This special relationship led to the church entering a deal with the Boy Scouts to screen, train and certify all people who worked with children. Upon hearing this, I immediately went to the pastor. I had already been through a background check and fingerprinting, as I had worked with the kids for several years.

"You still have to go through the Boy Scout training and certification." He said. This posed a huge problem for me because the Boy Scouts did not, at that time, allow gay people to work with kids. They didn't allow gay Boy Scouts.

"What do I say when I am asked the questions," I asked pastor. "I will not lie, so what is the church going to do?"

"You must take the training," he said. "We just won't tell them about your relationship."

I reluctantly went through the training that was taught by the Boy Scout leader at the church and a session member. How convenient. He handed me my ID card stating that I was certified by the Boys Scouts of America to work with children. Fancy that. I am sure I must be the only lesbian in the country to hold that distinction. *Wow, our church just told a big lie just to save a few bucks.*

The pastor could not even find a suitable place to display the plaques we won at the many competitions. I still have them. The meeting only served to make things worse. They did not like the mirror that I held up in front of them. They held their own position that I was too sensitive and misunderstood the events around me. *So twisted.*

There was a problem at church where a child was accused of molesting another child in the bathroom. Somehow, for a short time this was my fault. I wasn't even there, and they tried to say I wasn't watching the kids and that was why it happened.

Then there was the time that the Sunday school coordinator did not show up for church school, and the children were forced to wait outside without supervision for quite some time, I was told. Because of this, there was no Sunday school that day. At the staff meeting that followed, I was blamed for this. Pastor described what happened. I had no idea what was going on because the Dove Choir was singing that day, so at the time in question I was getting kids into robes and rehearsing their songs.

His description of the events was immediately followed by: "Leticia, why didn't you let the children into the Sunday school?" I could not believe my ears. "It was your responsibility to meet the church school children and let them in the building."

"That has never been one of my responsibilities," I fired back.

"The children were left alone, locked outside the building," he pushed back.

"That is not my job," I repeated. "It is not my job to unlock the education building or to greet the Sunday school children."

"Where were you this morning?" This man was relentless.

"I was where the choir director should be, in the choir room getting the choir ready for service. I had nothing to do with the operation or coordination of Sunday school. I applied for that position, and you gave it to someone else. I suggest you call and ask her where she was."

Not one other person said a word about this.

Shortly after this meeting in October 2011, things really took a turn to the dark side. Satan was working overtime. I had written the script for the Christmas pageant, the Nativity through the eyes of Joseph. We had already begun working on the Christmas music, and parts had been cast. I received an email from a church member telling me not to bother coming to the Sunday school to do music with the children. In addition to this turn of events, I was informed that the Christmas program that I directed would not be part of the 4:00 p.m. Christmas service, as it had always been. Instead, we were to have a stand-alone Christmas program/pageant on a different date. *There would be no 4:00 p.m. Christmas program?* This was very strange and stressful. It meant many more hours of work for the kids and me. However, I did as I was told and set out to make the changes.

Then yet another change, I was told that there would not be a Christmas pageant outside the service. Later, I received an email from the wife of a church member who told me not to bother coming to Sunday school to do music with the kids. She explained that she was doing the regular Christmas program at the 4:00 p.m. service, and I was welcome to help her. *Are you following this crazy mess? That loud sound you just heard was my head exploding again. Could I have been any angrier?* I decided to leave.

All of this was followed by several meetings in which there was a very slight admission that I may have been treated badly. At one point, I walked out of the meeting because the pastor kept lying, even after I called him out in front of the other attendees. After talking with another member, I returned to the meeting. We agreed to start fresh. There would be a member or members that I could come to if there were any further problems. Well, that was really a sweet fairytale. Not long after, I wrote:

TO: Session and Clergy,

I am sure this letter is expected.

You, the session or your member representatives and Carl, had two very long meetings with me. We came to an agreement to move

*forward in good faith and trust with clear parameters and expecta-
tions. I changed my decision to leave and agreed to continue to direct
the Dove and Praise Choirs. Clearly my trust was misplaced.*

*Immediately after we came to this agreement and I agreed to stay,
you made the decision to fire me as director of the Dove Choir. Then
you waited to tell me until after the Christmas holiday so you would
be sure I directed the planned 7:00 p.m. Christmas Eve Service. You
were so vindictive and in a hurry to punish me for speaking up for
myself and telling the truth about what really happened with the
Church School, that you did not even consider the children. You simply told me the day before rehearsal to cancel Dove Choir until my
replacement can be found. You could have waited till the end of the
choir year in June, which would have had less of an impact on the
children. I am told you will advertise. I am sure you already know
who my replacement is. I think I have just witnessed one of the most
unchristian things I have ever seen a collective body of Christians do.*

*I have seen and heard all manner of things at this church. I have been
referred to as a lawn jockey and humiliated with public comments
at the church regarding sexual acts. I have had a staff person angrily
throw a bulletin at me during a church service. I have had several
people tell outright lies about me for their own purposes and to cover
up their own mistakes. There is much more. In fifteen years many
other things have occurred that are too numerous to mention. I have
endured fifteen years of institutional racism and the humiliation that
comes with it. However, that the governing body of this church could
act in such a mean-spirited way and with such reckless disregard and
compassion for any member of the church is just reprehensible. The
clear disparity in treatment is blinding.*

*Effective January 18, 2012, I resign my position as director of the
Praise Choir, giving you much more notice and consideration than
you have given me. It is my intent to leave this church completely
including church membership. By this date, kindly remove me from
all lists, mailings, email lists, and membership roles.*

God bless you all.

On this same day, January 4, 2012, they fired me. They did not let me work out my two weeks' notice. Could it be that they didn't want me leaving on Martin Luther King's birthday? That would have been my last service, and we already had a special program of music planned for that service. Think of the optics of the only black member being forced out of the church on this holiday. Carl, the pastor, called me on my cell phone and summoned me to his office. He called me out of a rehearsal. I walked down the hall to his office. A session member was with him. Carl did all the talking. The session member just put his head down.

Carl said, "Effective right away you are fired. You must pack your things, turn in your keys, and leave immediately."

I do not know why I was so shocked, but I was. I didn't fall apart in front of Carl. I smiled and said, "No problem. You finally got what you wanted all along. But how do you really fire someone who already quit?"

I walked out the door. I barely functioned. I went back to the choir room where they were waiting for me to proceed with the rehearsal. They asked what music I wanted them to take out. I said, "I guess none. Carl just fired me and I should pack now."

They mostly packed. People made calls to husbands and friends who brought boxes. Most of us cried. I couldn't move. I was lost for a time. I had never been fired before. I had never been told to leave a church, certainly not my own church. It was surreal. But the pain was like nothing I ever experienced. It had more to do with the church than me. It was that a man of God had created and executed this Godless situation.

I lost my church, I lost people in my life, some of whom just seemed to blindly believe what they were told about me, keeping any questions they may have had to themselves or close friends. I had pain in places that people could never understand or reach. After all, this was my church family. My funeral service would have been in this church. These people are Christians, and a lot of what had happened involved lies and underhanded actions in a church where I was supposed to be safe. Where was the Christianity? Where was the Christ-centered church? Where was the love? I cried for one hundred days and one thousand tomorrows, sometimes not knowing why. I was not angry with God. The church was not God. Thank God! I knew God would get me through this pain. There is a difference between spirituality and religion, huge difference.

That week, Carl, the pastor, wrote a full-page letter explaining his version of why I left. He had it printed and distributed in addition to posting it on the Internet. He also gave others verbal explanations. He said that I did not work well with others and that I refused to teach the desired curriculum. *That would be about Jesus, right?* Plus, I did not teach Sunday school. And was never given a curriculum. I taught music. I also did not share his vision. Well, one must have a vision to share one. Still lies. I was gone and still he was not happy. He had to try to destroy my reputation.

He had made it most difficult for me to maintain a Christian outlook where he was concerned. I have often said that Point Pleasant Presbyterian Church would never prosper as long as he was the pastor. I heard they had moved to one service because attendance was low. Carl was blaming it on trends. All churches were supposedly losing people and suffering. Not true, not all churches. You have to plant the right seeds and water them with love not hate, positive not negative. It is hard to have a Christ-centered church without Christ.

Oddly enough, sometime later, I found myself in a local hospital in the Intensive Care Unit. Across the hall in the same ICU was Pastor Carl. His wife popped in to see me. I believe that God was at work here. I took the opportunity to tell her to tell her husband that I forgave him. I knew she would tell him. She was a pastor herself and understood the importance of my request. I never heard from him.

Weeks later, I was still in the rehab attached to the Medical Center, and he was still in the hospital or had returned. I had Donna take me in my wheelchair to his room. He looked as if he had seen a ghost.

"Hi Carl. I am out for a ride and heard you were here, so I stopped by. How are you feeling?"

He picked his mouth up off the floor and told me of his health issue. "My wife is coming, and maybe you will see her," he said.

"Maybe, but I best be getting back to my own room. Take care," I said.

I don't know why I expected an apology. I wanted to believe there was an ounce of remorse, an ounce of true Christianity in this man. He was a pastor and a politically connected big shot in the Presbytery. I am never getting that apology, and it is okay.

I used to read the email below from time to time just to remind myself that I am not crazy, and Christians really did this stuff to me. I received this email from a church member and friend whose daughter was in both choirs that I directed. She grew out of the Doves and into the Praise Choir.

> Don't u know that people believe in u? Have Faith in u? LOVE you?? Of course their allegiance is with you. We will all follow you wherever u go. Loyalty does NOT lie with Carl or Linda or Kim. The Bickerman's were acting upon Carl's direction—make no mistake—as I know they r HUGE fans of yours. Carl has tried to dick u out of the Xmas show every year! This year is no different. For whatever reason he is not a fan of yours, yet when people publicly support you of course he has to jump on that bandwagon. How would it look if he didn't??

> Since I have known u and been a part of this Church, he has undermined u and caused u unjust stress every time. U r always the scapegoat, the troublemaker, the non-team player, etc. The Xmas pageant, the boy scout drama, Joanne, Kim, not allowing u to run the school, Bill, money, countless nasty grams. It has to stop and I believe the best retribution u can have is to leave him high and dry with a very pissed off congregation.

I have so many more stories about this time in my life at this church, but I think now it is best I leave them in my past. I am grateful for the people I still hold dear to my heart. And I know there are gifts wrapped up in this experience.

Love is a Fruit of The Spirit

WELL, IT IS ABOUT TIME. THANK YOU, PRESIDENT OBAMA! ON June 26, 2013, the Defense of Marriage Act became history. This major turn of events was just what Marriage Equality supporters in New Jersey needed to boost their well-fought battle for same sex marriage. On September 27, 2013, a NJ judge cited the Supreme Court decision and declared that gay marriage should be legal in this state and ordered the State of New Jersey to allow same sex marriage beginning October 21, 2013. If there was ever a reason for a party—not that we needed a reason—this was it.

Donna and I waited more than thirty years for this. I used to say, what's in a word?

I feel married in every way that matters. In fact, at one point, I thought that I couldn't be any more married. But, the longer we were together, I had a sense that being legally married and all that goes with it, was very important on so many levels. It has an effect psychologically, socially, emotionally, economically, on every aspect of your day-to-day life.

Yes, we immediately started to plan our wedding. Just the decision to get legally married and have a wedding made a difference in our life together. I can't explain it exactly, but it was different than getting our domestic partnership and different from getting our civil union. It felt different. Perhaps it was a sense of equal validation. Our marriage would have the same standing as every other marriage.

So, when someone asks, "What's in a word?" tell them, "Everything."

To celebrate, we did one of our favorite things, Atlantic City. We had tickets to see Wolfgang Puck at the Borgata. We arrived and went to our favorite slot machine, *Sex and the City*, to play a bit before the program. We were not big fans of the show, but loved the game.

Wolfgang was very entertaining, but I was disappointed that he did not offer samples of what he cooked. By the middle of the demonstration, I was so tired. I didn't feel well. Donna asked about waiting in line to buy Wolfgang's book and to get his autograph. Normally, I would be right there. However, I declined and didn't even want to eat dinner at my favorite buffet at the Golden Nugget.

"Let's go home," I said. "I don't feel right."

"Are you sick?" Donna asked.

"No, not yet," I replied, "but I must be coming down with something. I am so tired. I just don't feel right."

So we left. All the way home, we talked about our wedding plans and all the preparation that needed to be done. We were in another dimension that transcended everything. When we got home, it was early, but we went right to bed.

The next morning, Donna and I were in the Emergency Room at Ocean Medical Center. I was weak, my speech seemed like it was changing. I didn't feel well.

"What seems to be the problem?" the doctor asked as he examined me.

"I think I am having a stroke," I answered.

"I think you're right," he responded.

That is the last thing I remembered with any clarity for a while.

The doctors told Donna that there wasn't much hope. I am not sure if that was before or after they made her leave me to go get our civil union papers to prove our relationship. Yes, they went there at a critical and devastating time like that. They would not take her word that we were a couple, even though she brought me there and was clearly genuinely concerned and upset. Donna was able to answer all their questions, as only a spouse could. How often do you think that straight couples are asked to produce a marriage license to medical staff at a time like that?

The doctor, clearly uncomfortable, asking for this document and proof, stated, "It is not me asking. It is hospital policy." Good thing for them that I was near death and not conscious when this happened.

Our friends helped make calls as Donna was devastated and could barely call the kids. Jeremy and Shawn were on the first flights home from Denver and Seattle, respectively, and Jayson hit the road immediately, driving up from Florida. Friends and family gathered. I am told that the doctors met with Donna, the boys and our friend, Cynthia, who at the time pretended to be Donna's sister so that she could be there to help Donna who was in shock. Of course she was in shock. One day, we were planning our wedding, and the next the doctors were requesting her signature on a Do Not Resuscitate form.

The doctors explained that it was not likely that I would survive. However, if I did survive, I would be a vegetable. I would need total care and would not speak or ambulate. I would have little brain function. Total darkness. No hope at all. *Just pull the plug now* is what they were saying. The covering doctor, who didn't know me at all, wrote in my chart that I would not want to live like that. How do you make that declaration without a signed DNR?

Shawn broke the dark silence that draped the meeting like a shroud. "Hell no! You don't know Leticia Walker. You don't know my mom. She's a fighter."

Meeting adjourned. Our friend, Michael, called and also told Donna, "Don't listen to the doctors; it is too soon to decide anything."

Back in the ICU, I lay motionless in a hospital bed. I was unconscious and not able to open my eyes.

Jayson said, "She needs music. There's no music."

He went back to the house and made a CD of some of my favorite songs and songs I had written and sung. The music played constantly. Friends and family held hands and prayed. Believers and non-believers prayed together for me. I would later learn that people that I didn't even know from places I had never been were praying for me.

I heard someone say they were going to give me propofol. I could not tell them no. I couldn't open my eyes or speak. However, I am told that at one point my monitors went wacky. I think that was me being upset that they were killing me like Michael Jackson, or so I thought.

My friend and drummer, Chuck, came to visit. He put a small wooden cross in my hand, "Do you know what is happening?" he asked.

I did; I was dying. I had no concept of time. There were moments when I had thoughts and then nothing. At times, I could hear, then silence. But always, there was music.

Two days later after my admission to Ocean Medical Center, I opened my eyes. I saw friends and family, but was most taken by the daylight coming from the window behind them. I had been in darkness for two days. The light soothed my soul. I was very weak and on a respirator. I was alive but not sure of anything. I could think and understand. I could hear. I could communicate with help from picture and word boards. I needed someone to help me lift my left hand and move in on the boards. My right side was not moving at all. I wondered how long I would live. I saw all the monitors and machines around me. There was a needle in my arm and bandages. During this time, I received a tracheotomy and a feeding tube.

After everyone left, I started talking to God. I prayed. I told God that I needed a little more time. I wanted time for Donna and I to be together, a vacation. I wanted to take her on a vacation. She deserved that, and for some time I was too busy working, teaching, directing, singing, performing. I wanted her to know, without a doubt, how very much I love her. I wanted to be sure that she would be okay. I wanted more time with my kids, family time. I wanted to take that family vacation to Disney that I always planned but never seemed to work out. I wanted to finish the three CD's I started, especially the gospel one. I prayed for stronger faith. I had moments of fear that I didn't understand.

Christians aren't supposed to fear anything. I don't think I feared death. I feared being without the ones I love. I didn't want to leave them. The music started to sound a bit different, like slow motion. I thought the time was near. I began praying for fearless faith, trusting God more. Later, the music was back to normal. It would do this several times. It sounded like death, then it sounded normal.

I could see what looked like old time folk parading down a road singing like Mardi Gras, joyfully singing and strutting, some doing a cakewalk. It also reminded me of the movies *Meet Me in St Louis* or *Easter Parade*. The people were dressed in that style. The visual I had was very clear, colorful and beautiful. Then the picture would fade, changing like the music.

This cycle was interrupted by the news that I was being moved to a specialty rehab because of my tracheotomy. Reality hit me. God saves my life every day and always has. I thought it might be a good idea to marry Donna in the hospital, so that she would have some legal protections. Then I realized that God brought us this far. *I will trust that we will marry on the date we planned, September 21, 2014.*

The CCU at Ocean Medical in Brick was a palace compared to this rehab located inside a hospital in Lakewood. It was a very drab and dingy place. There was very little light, even during the day. It was also crowded with stuff sitting around. They were always short staffed and a few of the staff, including nurses, were abusive. I had no problem filing a complaint about this when I was able to.

Our friend Lorrie came to visit me. It was so nice to see her. Lorrie is a book illustrator and graphic artist who is very creative. She made me a video using one of the songs off my cd. It was beautiful. The video was a collection of different flowers, mostly purple ones at different stages of their life cycle. There was an endless field of lavender and gorgeous purple roses. Some seemed to open before my eyes. It meant so much to me.

She also brought her iPad with her to help with communication. She held it for me and tried to help me write. It was difficult and took forever. I was trying to tell her what it was like to have a stroke. With help from Donna she was able to understand what I was trying to tell her. I was explaining that having a stroke was like being bitch slapped with a pair of Jimmy Choo shoes. Later, I was able to explain that I saw blood rushing at some point during the stroke. I felt like I was being beaten from head to toe, tumbling head over heels. Jimmy Choo shoes have a distinctive blood red bottom. I saw red.

While at this rehab, I was very focused on two people that were part of my reality but not real. These people were like the folks in the old American Gothic pictures, a man and his pitch fork and, in my view, a little black padre hat. The woman was very plain and heavyset with her hair in a bun and big apron. She looked like a sumo wrestler, but German. They, along with Donna would not feed me. I desperately wanted tea and french fries. I knew these people were just being mean because that's the kind of cold people they were. But Donna, how could she starve me when she knew I wanted french fries so badly. She kept talking crazy, saying that I was not allowed to have anything by mouth per the doctor. So now these two gothic folks had everyone on their side.

Then the mean people told me that Christ was coming, and they had to get ready for a celebration. We argued over this for almost a week. I told them that if Christ was coming, he would be staying at our home, which was a gift from him and also everyone knows that any party for Christ would be at our house because everyone knows that our house is the party house. These two kept interfering and trying to force their old conservative, twisted views and ways on me, even misquoting the Bible. Ok, I was out of it, but I could see them as well as I could see the back of my hand. *Crazy, right?* It wasn't drugs, it was dehydration.

There were nights I was afraid to fall asleep for fear I wouldn't wake up. There were times all of this seemed like a dream, a bad dream. There was always a nurse, needle, or treatment to remind me that the nightmare was real life. Finally, I was off the respirator and without a Trach. I was speaking. Thank you, God!

Eventually, they sent me to Shore Rehab, which is attached to the hospital. Two days later, I was back in the hospital because my kidneys were failing, and I was dehydrated. *Really!* I was in a medical facility, three different ones for five weeks. How did I get dehydrated enough to cause kidney failure? I have a theory. However, I will give this advice. Make sure someone is giving you liquids, if not by mouth, then through your feeding tube. I was able to survive this setback and was again admitted to Shore Rehabilitation. Therapy was tough.

One of God's many gifts to me, was my therapist, Mary. I affectionately referred to her at times as Merciless Mary. Nothing could be further from the truth. I presented a huge challenge, and Mary was more than up to the task. She skillfully acknowledged in her sessions with me that I was a total person and that my arms and legs and everything in between were involved in my success. I never heard her say this or that is an Occupational Therapy issue. She worked closely with OT and incorporated the overlap in my treatment.

While knowledge, skill, professionalism and implementation are keys to successful treatment, all of which Mary had an abundance of, Mary had a level of compassion, practicality and relatability that she integrated in her treatment but never let interfere with the goal or desired outcome. This was evident in the many times she listened to me vent about the issues I was having upstairs in the residence, but continued and never skipped a beat in treatment. As she listened, she continued to give me direction. She never let me slide.

I remember complaining and not wanting to move my leg. It was hard and uncomfortable.

Mary looked me in the eye and said exactly what I needed to hear. She said, "Tish, you had a stroke and have been in bed a long time, it's going to hurt, if you want to walk again, it's not going to be easy."

It was clear to me that pain would be involved in my recovery, but I felt safe in her very capable hands. She allowed me to cry when I needed to but never let me wallow. I would often cry and repeat, "I can do all things through Christ who strengthens me." Sometimes, it felt like she cried and prayed with me.

She instinctively knew when I needed a break and when I didn't. This was evident when, during my break, she would give me yet another task. The most important thing Mary did for me was what she didn't do. She never once said, "You are never going to walk again." Even though she knew all odds were against it, and she may have thought it, she never questioned my faith or took away my hope. I also had occupational and speech therapy for a few sessions. Speech was not a big issue for me. Thank you, God.

After two long months and a few days, I went home. They wanted to place me in a sub-acute, kind of a nursing home, but I knew that was a bad idea. I still needed a lot of intense therapy. I would not get that in a sub-acute. I was happy to go home.

I was forever changed by this experience. I had a lot of time to reflect. Donna was with me some part of every day, sometimes the entire day from my admission to my release. Friends came from far and near to see me. There were visits from members of the group I direct and my students—multiple visits. They sang to me and polished my nails. Friends washed my hair and brought me sweet smelling lotions and soaps. They brought lunch for me and Donna and joined us. I received beautiful flowers, poinsettias, and an endless supply of purple. One could not imagine the acts of love that were shown to me. The outpouring of love was wonderfully overwhelming. I had friends that I didn't know I had. I saw my friends in a different light. I have always said that I love my friends, truly love them. With that love, comes risk. But it is worth the risk.

Love is the single most important thing there is and God's greatest gift to us, on so many levels, in so many ways. Love is the bridge, the common denominator. It is the Godly human connection. When you have love of any nature, you have everything. It is peace. It is freeing. Love is a fruit of the Holy Spirit. I love my God. I love my family and my friends. I found a deeper understanding of God's grace, God's love, God's favor, blessings, and anointing.

I have been abundantly blessed. I know first-hand that through Christ all things are possible. Prayer does change things. God does answer prayer, and the sun will come out eventually. And even if it rains, sometimes the rain and the sound of rain beating down is so beautiful. Rain is true soul music by God. It is such a beautiful day, even when it rains. You don't need the sun to define a beautiful day. You just have to see the miracle in the vision. You just have to see the gift.

Kiss Me in the Sunlight

JANUARY 30, 2014 WAS A VERY COLD BUT SUNNY DAY. AS WE DROVE away from the rehab that had been my home for two months, I realized that, including my hospital stay and my time in the Trach rehab, I had not seen the streets we were driving on or my home for three months. I noticed that the streets were wet. There were still mounds of snow along the roads, even though the sun was so bright. Driving down the roadways, I saw familiar sights that now somehow seemed unreal, almost mystical. I could not help but think, *I never thought I would see this again.* When we drove down our street, I noticed some leaves and the trees. I will never complain about the leaves again. I had in the past. They fell everywhere and got in the pool, often clogging the filter. Now they seemed more like a gift than a problem. I was glad to see what autumn had left behind. Our street was tree-lined and our property was overgrown with trees that had a visual impact even in winter. Yes, I was very happy and grateful to see the trees.

I was mostly quiet on the ride home, somewhat balancing between shock and awe. *I am home; thank you, Jesus. I am home.* I was reminded in that moment of the absolute power of God. After all, by all accounts I was supposed to be dead or at the very least a vegetable. Clearly, God had other plans for me. I wish doctors would stop practicing medicine and finally learn the skill. Then they would be more in touch with what God is doing.

I remember one of my doctors saying to me, "I thought you were toast," then added, "I never took into account your faith."

Maybe that is what is blocking the learning and why doctors are practicing still. We all need God. Life and death is still His domain. So doctors, do your job, but stay in your own lane.

Donna said very little and let me process the enormity of the situation. I sat in my wheelchair and looked out the sliding glass doors at the yard, past the pool and around what I always called *the lower forty.* It was really just a few acres of mostly trees. I was happy to be home yet uncomfortable in my own home. As I looked out, tears came.

Donna hugged me and said, "I am so happy you are home. I was so afraid of losing you. I couldn't. What would I do without you?"

We both cried a bit. I was still weak with little stamina, so Donna helped me into the hospital bed that was now next to the fireplace in the family room. Of course, we would not be using the fireplace even though it was winter because of the changes in the room. I did miss a warm fire and hot tea on a cold winter night.

I hated the hospital bed. It was very uncomfortable and depressing. The only positive was that it was a bit bigger than a single bed, so Donna could squeeze in to visit me a while before she went to the airbed across the room. There was no way we could comfortably be in that bed together for even one hour. That may have been the worst part, if there was a worst part. My hemiplegia, partial paralysis, made it very hard to hug and hold, something we did a lot of BICH, *Before IntraCranial Hemorrhage. Wow, kind of funny, BICH. The T is missing, but the stroke was a bitch, so it works.*

It was a long, hard road I traveled, trying to get back to me, and I am still on it. After I left the rehab, therapy continued with new therapists. I learned a new and different dance, three steps forward, two steps back, not my favorite, but I was getting good at it. I was always ahead by at least one step. It is a process. So this was my life: a hospital bed, therapy and doctors. *I don't think so. This is so not me.* By late March, I decided that the hospital bed had to go. It made me feel like I was still in rehab and helpless. I learned to love and live with my recliner. I was so happy to have my friend and extremely skilled chiropractor, Dr. Robert Crystal, on my team before and after my IntraCranial Hemorrhage. He visited and adjusted me weekly, after I came home from the rehab. A doctor who makes house calls, he is such a gem.

My new occupational therapist, Rachelle, helped me so much by strengthening my weaknesses and by applauding my strengths. She, like Mary, was also a blessing from God. He sent so many good people to be in my corner. Rachelle incorporated my life into my therapy; therefore, even though she knew very little about the technical side of music, conducting was part of my therapy. We talked about my love for cooking, so functioning in the kitchen became part of my therapy. But the coolest therapy session ever was a surprise even to me.

I went for my regular therapy session and noticed that we were set up a little differently. There was a full-length mirror on the other side of the therapy table and more space to work in than usual. *Ugh,* I thought, *she is going to put me through it today.* I sat on the therapy table waiting for my therapist, and she appeared right on time with a colorful but odd-looking bunch of something. She handed me a bouquet of flowers made from pipe cleaners.

She said, "It is time we start working on that walk down the aisle you keep talking about."

So we did. Talk about going the extra mile! It would be tricky because I would be holding the bouquet of flowers in my left hand. This meant no cane. Any additional support would come from my son who would walk me down the aisle. We worked on this until I felt comfortable. I am sure it looked odd for others in the therapy gym to see my therapist and I—two women— walk down the aisle together, with me holding my beautiful hand-made pipe cleaner bouquet. This meant so much to me.

There was a lot of preparation for that big day. It was so much more than a wedding. It was a celebration of life, of beating the odds, not just as a couple but also medically. I was told that only thirteen percent of people survive what I had been through. It was love wins in every way. I set out to get to work but very quickly remembered that I had limitations. Our friend, Ann, jumped in to help. She was very organized. What I couldn't do online, she handled with some help from some members of the bridal party. Of course, the color scheme had to include and be dominated by the color purple. Anyone who knows me would expect that—purple and pastel green. The colors were so pretty together, and green is one of Donna's favorite colors.

The whole process was very traditional. There were five females with male counterparts in the wedding party. Even though our ages were on the upper side of the tote board, we were no different than a bridal party in their twenties. We had a traditional rehearsal dinner, although I nearly lost it at the suggestion that the girls wear tuxes. That is so not us. We shopped for gowns, bickered about accessories and decorations. The men were not very interested in the details. Still, we had the best bridal party ever for many reasons.

My best person was my friend, John. We have been friends for close to forty years, and John was with Donna and I when we started our journey together. Donna chose a childhood friend, Karen, to stand with her. The remainder of the group included my sister, who is also named Donna, and our friends Ann, Marilyn, Sharyn, Ron, Mike, Drew, and Wayne.

We had a workday to make decorations that turned out beautifully with lights, some sort of grass, wine glasses, and purple marbles floating in water. We put together the purple covered Bibles, joined with a white flower and ribbons, that the women would carry as they walked down the aisle.

The gowns were tasteful, elegant and purple. Each woman chose the style of gown that looked best on her. Then we had the gowns made from the same fabric. Donna bought her wedding outfit at Lord and Taylor's. It was gorgeous. It was a silky, cream-colored top with accordion bell sleeves with silky flowing pants to match. She wore a 1960s flower child type headpiece with flowing ribbons off the back. I had a purple gown made for myself with a white jeweled floor-length duster. I purchased a floor-length veil that I attached to my tiara.

The fellas wore black suits with purple matching ties. Todd and Gianna, two of my students, served as ring bearer and flower girl. Our son, Shawn, was the officiant. Jeremy and Jayson walked the brides down the aisle. The actual ceremony was in an outdoor garden area that was tastefully and celestially decorated by the bridal party.

It was awesome even with a few mishaps. For example, the sandals I wore had no support, unlike the shoes that I had practiced in. The length of my gown also became an issue as I was tripping on it on my way down the aisle. Lastly, the aisle was cobblestone as the wedding was in an outside area of the banquet hall. This was completely different terrain from the floor in the therapy gym. Also, the DJ screwed up the music some, and the ring bearer went down the aisle without music.

Nevertheless, I did make it down the aisle with help, crying most of the way, and stood for our vows. I heard the music of John Legend's *All of Me*. Everyone stood as the brides came down the aisle. Donna was first. She was a vision of love and clearly happy.

As I came down the aisle I saw that some people were crying with me. Everyone understood the enormity of the moment. When I made it down past the people, just before I got to Donna, who was waiting tearfully for me to get to her, there was an explosion of applause. This was an accomplishment eclipsed only by the wedding itself.

Ten months earlier, I wasn't expected to live. Yet, on this day I was marrying the person that I had shared my life with for thirty-three years. The word celebration doesn't cover it. Our friend, Cynthia, called it the wedding of the century, and it was. On this day, love was in the air and all around. It was palpable. People spoke about it. God was there. Well, God is everywhere, but on this day, it was more than that.

There were three readings from the Bible and a collage of Maya Angelou's writings read during the ceremony. There were prayers and music, yes, music. *Collective Joy* sung joyously, and the recorded music for the processional and recessional was spot on. The bridal party walked down the aisle to *Forever*, a song I had written for Donna a while back. We exited the area hearing Stevie Wonder sing, *I'll be loving you always*! Very fitting.

"Therefore, what God has joined together . . ."

Yes, he did join us together. I asked and I received. God does answer prayer. I asked for someone who would truly love me and whom I would truly love in return. I suppose some folks would say that I should have been gender specific in my prayer request. Frankly, it never occurred to me. No one was more surprised than I at the unexpected answer to my prayer. Clearly, God wasn't concerned about the gender issue either. The operative word in the prayer request was love, which is who and what He is.

God is love. Love is the basis for everything. That is what God teaches us. I learned without knowing I was being educated. It doesn't matter whom you love, only that you love. Love, what a tremendous gift.

Donna, what a tremendous gift.

Love Saved Me

I HAVE BEEN BLESSED IN MY LIFE TO KNOW LOVE AND TO HAVE love in so many ways, such as through God, family, romance, and friendships. Donna and my children are among God's many magnificent gifts to me. I say among because there are so many more.

How crazy that I spent most of my life watching and waiting, looking for God to bless me in a way that would make up for the very unpleasant and painful moments during my life.

We are told that God will give us beauty for ashes, so I waited. As I waited, many blessings and gifts came to me, and I was grateful; but I still wanted the big house, although I already had one, a nice car, although I already had one. I also had friends, family, friends I called family, and more. I didn't see it. I was waiting to win the lottery or win big at a casino. I wanted to help my family and do wonderful things for my friends. I wanted to start programs that would help people. I wanted my own studio. I wanted to help the world. Imagine my surprise when I realized that God had more than given me beauty for ashes. He gave me love in so many different ways, and it was God's love that saved me throughout my life.

I have been taught, and I believe that God so loved the world, that he gave us his son. There is no greater love than this. He gave us salvation and forgiveness, a chance to make wrongs right. He gave us a do-over. Every day is a do-over. This is the gift of all-encompassing love.

Looking back, I see that my mother made sure that I knew about kindness, that God loves me, and all that goes with it. Her mantra, *God first, others second, and me last,* was so ingrained that it might as well have been seared onto my body like a cattle brand. My mother strives to live love. That is why she, without a thought, let a stranger who knocked on our door share our Christmas. My mother may not have always made the best decisions or, over the years, understood the complexities of the times, and she often stated her misunderstandings as fact. But she was always clear on one thing: God!

My father, however, made it clear that he did not love me. I was a total disappointment at birth because I was a girl. From my father's point of view, Mom struck out twice as I had an older sister. Why was it so important for him to have a boy? Mind you, my father had many other issues that had an impact on his marriage, the least of which was his propensity to be so generous with his penis. Just because you can, doesn't mean you should.

I do not love my father as a daughter loves her father. I do not love my father because of a biological relationship. I love him as part of humanity because we should all love one another. It has always been clear to me that my mom loved me, and my father didn't. Now I understand the reason is that my mother has a relationship with the Lord and is a spiritual woman. My father was a Godless man. I believe that you have to know God on some level to know love of any kind. Love is a gift to us from God. If you have a sense of God, a connection to the universe, then you are innately able to love. I believe we are all born with this connection. Some people, for whatever reason, get disconnected.

Fortunately, my mother was so connected that she could give me love for two, so I never really missed having a father. I doubt that I would have visited him at all were it not court mandated. You can't miss what you never had. I forgive my father for not loving me and for the sexual and emotional abuse.

I was also blessed with God's love through my sister, Catherine, who passed on way too early. We tend to think that our time together has no limits. *I will call her tomorrow. I will visit next week.* It doesn't occur to us that there may not be a next week as we go about our day to day activities. I honored her with love in the best way I could. I sang her favorite song, *I Could Only Imagine,* at her funeral. I don't know how I was able to do it. I only knew that I had to.

Life really is too short, and I have come to realize that it is not just a catch phrase. I have learned that no matter how long you live, some pain never stops hurting. This is especially true not only in the case of losing a loved one, but for other types of pain also, the pain of rape, for example. Still, with love, we learn to manage pain. You can't let yourself normalize abuse to the point that you get use to it and do not recognize it when it happens. That was a long hard lesson.

Seven years after my sister, Catherine's, death I found an envelope that she had sent to me postmarked March 2008. It was a birthday card. Yes, on the day before my birthday, seven years after she left us, I got a birthday card from her. Somehow this card had been misplaced all those years, and I never saw it. It was found lying out in the open on a table in the basement. This was odd because this table had been used many times and passed by many times, but the card was not there. Then it appeared out of the blue with a message of love. This is the memory I choose to keep of my sister and how I choose to remember her. The memory where she reminds me that she loved me.

Unsaid things and any other issues just do not matter. In the end, there is love. Love matters! Love is eternal.

I was blessed with my own children and, like all parents connected to and through the gift of love, innately loved my children. I love my sons in the most unadulterated and unconditional way. I love and am proud of the men they have become. It is unfathomable that this love could grow any larger, and I could love them any more, but somehow I do with each moment that passes. The day Donna legally adopted the boys legitimized our family to society and also gave us a tangible memento of our family bond.

Donna and I are so blessed in so many ways. Our kids have grown to be warm, sensitive, kind men, who are strong, intelligent and successful. I love our family. I love when the boys come home to visit. They all live out of state now. It is really cool when they are home at the same time. At our wedding, our son, Shawn, officiated, while Jeremy and Jayson gave me and Donna away. It was beautiful beyond belief. Not just the wedding, but also that family moment in time. I cherish the time that we are all together, Donna, me, and our three sons.

Donna is one of God's greatest gifts to our family and especially to me. I was in such a dark place at one time. I was in a relationship but still lonely and on a path of self-destruction. I was dying. My spirit was all but lost. I prayed to God for someone to love and who would love me. He sent me Donna. Love saved me. God's love for me saved me, and Donna's love for me saved me. Love lifted me! With Donna, I finally learned what love is.

That lesson was a long journey that included many twists and turns and misinterpretations of love. Because I had love—God's love—so deeply instilled in me, I took chances on love, or what I thought was love, in my life. The miracle of love is supplemented by our ability to reconnect to love, to God, if we've separated. Issues arise when people do not accept or want the gift of love. They do not realize how this decision impacts their life and darkens their path. Maybe some people are afraid of the outcome if they reach out or take a chance on love, like that song, *Taking A Chance On Love*. I took a huge chance on love with Ken for five years, however misguided.

Some of the risks I took on love have blossomed beautifully into wonderful friendships and/or loving relationships. Some did not. Some were painful and hurtful. (Please note: if you have to get out of bed to talk to your best friend, you married the wrong person.) So I came to truly understand that without the bad, we would never appreciate the good. Without the storm, we would not understand or appreciate the calm. Without sorrow, we would not know joy. Without darkness, love and the warmth of light, the true brilliance, would not be appreciated or understood.

One thing I came to understand is that learning what love isn't is part of learning what love is. My father, Peter, Ken, Ray have taught me some of what love isn't. People often confuse love with other things, sex, for example. That may be why we are taught to wait until after the wedding to have sex. Sex can muddy the waters. Good sex, coupled with a fun date, can give the illusion of true love. Tina made an excellent point when she sang, *What's love got to do with it?* You can surely have sex with people you don't love, and you can love a person and never have sex with them. I am sure that the men who abused me did not love me.

Sex is fleeting. I actually knew of a few couples that broke up because the sex didn't work for them anymore. I think two things about that: one, that is twisted, and two, they misunderstood their relationship from the start. Love finds a way to work it out. Even Ken and I, believing we had love, found a way to deal with his attraction to men. He just didn't stick to the plan. And as I said, I learned what love isn't.

When I met and started to date Donna, even though I had been around the gay community for some time, I was uncomfortable with the notion that when people looked at me or talked about me, I was now reduced to the woman who has sex with women and that this was a negative. Donna and I both came from relationships with men. However, we came to feel that some-how we now had a scarlet letter on us that some people could see and others speculated about.

It has always bothered me that society in general defines gays in terms of sex. Not what sex they are, but how much they have and with whom. If you ask most people what the definition of a gay person is, the usual response is a man who has sex with a man or a woman who has sex with a woman. That is all gays are and all gays do, if you ask some people. But we are all—gay or straight—so much more than sex. Sex is but a sliver of our total make up as humans. What about love? How about no labels or we define it as people who believe that it doesn't matter who you love only that you love?

Donna and I know it doesn't matter who you love. It is love that mat-ters. It is love that saves us. It saves us from ourselves. It saves us every day. When Donna was battling breast cancer and things were bleak, love saved me, and God saved Donna. When I lay unconscious near death in a hospital bed, God saved me. Love saved me. God's love comes to us with gifts of hope and faith if we accept them. Hope and faith are formidable instruments to help us in the face of adversity. Having faith in God doesn't mean that you will never face challenges. It means that if and when you do, you will have help with those challenges you face.

I am so glad that I continued to take risks. We should never close ourselves off from the possibility of love. Soon I will celebrate thirty-five years together with my gift from God, two years of which are now recognized by the US government as a legal marriage. Personally, I think they should back-date my marriage license, but I don't see that happening. Really, every day is a celebration. We should celebrate love every day. Love is eternal.

It is difficult to understand that a person wouldn't have even the smallest connection to love. Love is all around us. I see it in the night sky that sparkles brilliantly with the stars of heaven and the fullness of the moon. It is in a single snowflake that falls from the winter sky and touches our skin. I see love in the vast ocean and the ripples of a brook. It is in the tallest trees and the most delicate flowers. Love is seen in a baby's birth and a child's smile. It is in the sound of quiet and the resonance of sound. It is the reverberations of the universe. It is the music of life. It is the purpose of humanity.

I am sure most of us were exposed to or taught *love one another as I have loved you* and the Golden Rule, *do unto others as you would have them do unto you* . . . but I wonder how many people really live these universal lessons?

I look around and listen to the news. Often I wonder if some people ever heard of love or God in any context or fashion. I don't get Columbine, September eleventh or a mugging on the street. I don't get rape or homelessness. If you have a family, you should always have a home. This includes non-biological family. The value of a human life seems to have diminished greatly in our society. People have been killed for the newest sneakers, the latest cellphone and loose change. Where is the love? Racism, homophobia, and bigotry are born out of fear and fueled by ignorance. Hate is the outgrowth of this conundrum. Where is the love? The person at the Woolworth store and the people at the Country Club didn't know a thing about me. Still, there was a sting of racism and bigotry. Where is the love?

Sometimes it seems that the longer I live, the more questions I have and the more complicated the answers, if there are answers. Love is both complicated and simple at the same time. We may never fully understand the depths of God's love for us or love in general with its many facets and faces. But we have faith and hope to help us through the process. Love in all its different forms saved me, even in the face of adversity. All the time I waited; I had it all the time. Love!

In celebration of our twenty years together, I wrote this song. Our bridal party walked down the aisle to it. The song is as true today as the day I wrote it.

FOREVER

Another year has gone by still I'm mystified

We are here side by side forever

We've had our share of ups and downs

Yet here we stand on higher ground

Loving you loving life

Forever

And after all that we've come through

I want to end my days with you

I thank the lord each day for the gift he gave

When you came into my life forever

You bring me joy you ease my pain

You know for you I'd do the same

All we are all we share

Forever

And after all that we've come through

I want to end my days with you

I thank the lord each day for the gift he gave

When you came into my life forever forever

And after all that we've come through

I want to end my days with you

I thank the lord each day for the gift you gave

When you came into my life forever

And I I'll love you

Forever

I love your smile

It leads the way

It helps me through my day

You cheer me on

And bring me home

We share a love a love forevermore forevermore

The end.

VISIT **leticiawalker.com** AND FOLLOW
THE INSTRUCTIONS TO RECEIVE A
FREE COPY OF THE SONG "**FOREVER**"
PROMO CODE= LUCY921

Postscript

Some Things Need to Be Said.

I HAVE HAD A VERY DIFFICULT TIME WATCHING AND LISTENING TO the goings-on of this presidential election season. I am not seeing a lot of love, and I am hearing a lot of hate. As a person who has been sexually abused, I find this seemingly acceptable rape culture reprehensible, hurtful and dangerous. Locker room talk? Public figures are spewing hate like they are singing a song. They don't even try to hide it, and a lot of people are ok with it. This is scary!

Is there no limit to stupidity, hate? I am overwhelmed with thoughts of how some people just don't get it. They do not even try to understand love and the beauty of God's love. God put it out there for everyone in terms so simple a two-year-old could get it. Love, caring, and sharing; these are simple concepts. I don't get why some people don't get it. This country has an epidemic of bigotry, hate, greed, and an overall lack of compassion and empathy. This couldn't be any further from God's message of love, mercy and forgiveness. Kids are killing their parents. Governments are killing their people. Adults and children are killing each other for cellphones and cars. Life is treated like it has no value. People are breaking into homes and businesses and taking what is not theirs to take. Some people will lie for the sole purpose of hurting another or for their own personal gratification or gain, and then swear to God they are speaking the truth. Where is the love?

Then there are our Christian leaders, religious leaders, *yes I am going there*, who purport to be in Christ, who say they are men of God, then open their mouths and preach hate. Some of them try to hide it by using the Bible to try to justify their words and actions. I am not judging anyone. God will do that. What I am saying is, if you are going to profess to lead in the name of God, preach God's message and lead.

Stay out of politics. That is not your job, not your lane. Marriage between any two people is between them and God, not you, them and the government. Stop using the Bible to try to justify your personal feelings and beliefs. I am sick and tired of bigotry in the name of God. Let me remind you that God made us all: black, white, gay, straight, and everything in between. God loves us all. Stop hiding behind man's spin on the Bible that you know is not correct as it flies in the face of Christ's teachings. God gave us a brain to use. Use it for good, not harm. Clearly, He does not want us to be stupid.

Preach God's love for everyone. Leave the judging to God. Judging is not your place or lane either. Stay in your place. Stay in your lane. Preach that to your people. Many of them have followed you down a path away from God's message of love, giving, kindness, and compassion. If all the religious leaders in a neighborhood, a state, a country, actually taught and preached God's message, the world would be a much better place.

Let me put it in terms you, as clergy, often use when speaking to us. God will hold you accountable for what you teach and how you lead. I suggest you get His message right and get it out there, instead of preaching your sick, twisted lies and hate. You can heal the harm you have done; mend the hearts and fences that you have caused to break. You are standing at the crossroads of life appearing not to know the names of the streets. But you do know. Shed some light.

All that said, I love you and hope that everyone can see and feel the blessing of love!

Acknowledgments

THIS BOOK WOULD NOT HAVE BEEN POSSIBLE WITHOUT THE LOVE, support and encouragement of Donna Shields to whom I am eternally and whole-heartedly grateful.

My deepest gratitude goes to my three sons, Jayson, Shawn, and Jeremy, who make me proud and keep me humble every day of my life.

I would like to express my sincere gratitude to Dee Anderson, for her skills as a writing coach and her professional advice given in publishing this manuscript.

My sincere appreciation and thanks to Elizabeth Leonard for her thoughtful and laser sharp editing and her creativity as a teaching artist and writer.

My unending gratitude to Dey Studio and Lorrie Dey for her creative illustrations and cover design.

Special thanks goes to Jennifer Ann Davis for additional editing and for highlighting the importance of teachers.

Special thanks to Molly Glenn for her creativity and drawing for the back cover.

I would like to thank the following people for their comments during the process of writing this book: Donna Shields, Marilyn Mitchell, Keith Bradley, Donna Ferry, Wayne Verducci, Cynthia Youngman, Sandy Grebel, Andrea Grandinetti,

Jayson Simpson and Patrick Quaye.

Special thanks to Cherished Memories Plus, for the about the author photo taken by, Bruce Stephens.

I am grateful to my personal trainer, Matt Busacca, for so much. He trained me as though I was an athlete and not a stroke patient. Matt made me want to push harder and consider water ballet. I was devastated to lose you but as always you took care of me and gave me Taylor when you were promoted. Congratulations and thank you.

There are not enough words to express my gratitude to Taylor Gregory. He is truly a gifted personal trainer. This kind and compassionate man has helped me regain movement and strength that I was told were gone forever. He is also a talented guitarist and singer. I think we were a match from the start. It is Taylor who saw the possibilities and sent me to SOAR Physical Therapy.

I give a very special thanks to the folks at SOAR Physical Therapy. It is truly a place of healing. Their individual and hands on approach is just what I needed. My therapist there, Dr. Elizabeth Horton, is a kind, caring and skilled therapist. Her keen approach to evaluation and treatment has proven invaluable to my recovery and I am forever grateful.

My heartfelt gratitude goes to Dr. Robert Crystal, my chiropractor and friend. Thank you for being you. It was so comforting to look up and see you at my bedside in the hospital. Your knowledge of chiropractic care combined with your sweet spirit and healing touch is a perfect combination to do God's work. Thank you!

My sincere appreciation goes to the folks at Wyatt Physical Therapy. Wyatt specializes in lymphedema therapy. The knowledge and skill that they bring to the treatment of lymphedema is superior and proficient. The staff at Wyatt is very supportive. Please support their efforts to provide treatment to all who need it. Look them up on Facebook.

My interminable gratitude goes to Patrick X. Amoresano, Esq. whose expertise and support is profoundly appreciated. He cares deeply about justice and helping others. He is a unique individual, a lawyer with a heart of gold who hears you.

My unending gratitude goes to Dr. Judy L. Schmidt, MD FACP, who is the expert's expert. Her care, knowledge, skill and support are exceedingly appreciated. She is an extraordinary individual to whom I will be forever grateful.

I would be remiss if I did not thank my friend, Con Gallagher, who has repeatedly said over the years, "Leticia, you should write a book, and I would like the movie rights." Well, Con, I did it! And there is so much more to write about!

Every Monday for nearly 4 years, Marc Cohn has sat at my piano and played for me. Even when I had no ability to sing, he played and encouraged me to try to sing, first sounds, then scales, a bit of scat, and then a song. Thank you Marc for your generous spirit, your time and your friendship.

On Wednesdays comes my help. My band, The Help, Chuck Gianakos, Frank Genus, and Don Glenn are great guys and first rate musicians. I am grateful and honored to make music with you. Thank you! The life I love is making music with my friends. Thanks for waiting for me.

There are so many people to thank. If you did not read your name here, please know that I appreciate everything everyone has done for me, the love and support that I continue to receive, and I thank God for blessing me with such wonderful people in my life.

About the Author

LETICIA WALKER IS A DAUGHTER, MOTHER, GRANDMOTHER, A spouse, friend, a Christian, a singer, songwriter, choir director, a cook, teacher, student, and businesswoman, a Trekkie, a Fanilow, and more. Grounded in faith, she has a spiritual outlook toward life.

Walker is an accomplished songwriter and lyricist. Eight of the ten songs on her disc, *Forever*, are original and brought her international recognition. Walker has composed the music for a musical adaptation of Shakespeare's *A Midsummer Night's Dream* entitled, *Secrets of a Midsummer Night*. Her Christmas CD, *Christmas and All That Jazz*, and a gospel CD are in the works, and the long awaited *Exposed Heart* will follow. Leticia also coaches and teaches voice.

Walker founded and directed a local college choir and has enjoyed serving her church, working as a cantor and musical director. She appeared in the film *Winning Losers* as well as in concerts in New York City, Washington DC, and Philadelphia.

A passionate humanitarian, Leticia has lent her talents to support the March of Dimes, American Cancer Society, the fight against AIDS, Music Beats the Streets and Disabled American Veterans. Walker has also served as President of the Board of Directors for Rainbow's End and performed for this organization that brings entertainment to those in institutions, nursing homes and rehabilitation facilities.